It Takes a Village Idiot

Complicating the Simple Life

Jim Mullen

Simon & Schuster

New York   London   Toronto   Sydney   Singapore

SIMON & SCHUSTER
Rockefeller Center
1230 Avenue of the Americas
New York, NY 10020

Designed by Chris Welch
Manufactured in the United States of America

1   3   5   7   9   10   8   6   4   2

Library of Congress Cataloging-in-Publication Data
Mullen, Jim (Jim R.)
It takes a village idiot : complicating the simple life / Jim Mullen.
p.   cm.
1. Mullen, Jim (Jim R.)—Homes and haunts—New York (State)—Catskill
Mountains Region—Humor. 2. Catskill Mountains Region (N.Y.)—Social life and
customs—20th century—Humor. 3. Country life—New York (State)—Catskill
Mountains Region—Humor. 4. Mullen, Jim (Jim R.)—Homes and haunts—
New York (State)—New York—Humor. 5. Manhattan (New York, N.Y.)—Social life
and customs—20th century—Humor. 6. New York (N.Y.)—Social life and cus-
toms—20th century—Humor. 7. City and town life—New York (State)—New
York—Humor. 8. Catskill Mountains Region (N.Y.)—Biography. 9. Manhattan
(New York, N.Y.)—Biography. 10. New York (N.Y.)—Biography. I. Title.
F127.C3 M87 2001
974.7'38043'092—dc21   [B]   00-054784
ISBN 0-7432-1131-6

It Takes a
Village Idiot

THERE IS NOTHING TO DO IN WEEKEND LAND. It's sooooooo boring. Isn't that why we pay the big bucks to live in Manhattan? So we won't ever be bored? We're sure not getting any space for it. While we're here at the stupid beach slapping away seagulls, there are things going on in Manhattan.

"THESE PEOPLE WERE nice enough to invite us out to the Hamptons, and this is how you say thank you?"

"So I should shut up and act like a pod person?"

"No one expects you to improve *that* much. You could just act like a normal person," Sue whispered.

"If we were normal, they wouldn't have invited us out here. We'd be like everybody else. Nowadays being one in a million means that there are six thousand people out there exactly like us. People want us to be different."

"Fine. You want to do something different? Help me make the bed."

"I don't make the bed at home, I certainly don't want to make it now that I'm a guest."

"You don't want them to think you're a miserable slob, do you?"

"But I *am* a miserable slob."

"I know that and you know that, but *they* don't know that."

"They're going to wash the sheets as soon as we clear out, so what possible difference could it make?"

"Would you keep your voice down? If you'd get out of it, *I'll* make the stupid bed."

Which was not my point at all. My point was the idiocy of going away for the weekend.

We could be sitting in front of our own television, flipping through our own channels, watching Elsa Klensch wring answers out of Karl Lagerfeld and Issey Miyake on CNN with a string of merciless, hardball questions like, "Is length important?" "What about daytime?" "How do you feel about texture?" "Is gray this year's black?" But when you're visiting, you can't hog the TV. You're not expected to do anything so crass as turn it on.

After we've read the paper and seen the view and heard about who bought the house down the lane, I'm about ready to explode. I feel like the computer Hal in *2001* when the astronaut starts to take away his memory. Don't do it, Sue.

"I . . am . . . slowly. . . . losing . . . . . my . . . . . . mind."

The weekend houses all scream, "Look at me, I'm different," in a way that makes them all the same. In the kitchen there's a butcher-block island with a set-in pastry marble, an overhead rack dripping with Calphalon pots; there are triple stainless steel sinks, Spanish terra-cotta tiles on the floor. This is the heart of the house, where the meals will be made, where the family will come together and share the news of the day. The Little House on the Beach.

Of course, the family never eats there. The pots have dust on them. The two kids are up in their room smoking dope and playing video games. The parents are barely speaking to each other; the kids are barely speaking to the parents. The microwave and the trash compactor are the most used appliances in the house. The only time they cook is when there are visitors around like us. They pretend to be civil for the weekend, but on Monday neither Sue nor I would be shocked to get the phone call that they've decided to split up "amicably."

There's an eating area and a conversation area and a family area. I'm always afraid when I visit one of these places I'm going to have to pee in a bathroom area, some huge, blond space with lots of glass, with a big, hand-worked wooden hole in the center of the floor.

The master bedroom suite is bigger than our entire apartment. And cleaner. It has his and hers toilets with matching sinks, tubs, and showers. No doors. You get privacy by going through a maze of U-turns. Turn right, you fall into a Jacuzzi; turn left, you're in the steam room. There are dressing rooms and exercise rooms, all wired for cable TV and phones.

The whole point is to have more, not less. Why scrimp? Let other people, the people with only one small Manhattan apartment, scrimp.

It is the typical New Yorker's dream house, totally customized, every detail agonized over. Notes jotted down in the middle of the night, then endless hours of discussion. The walls have been painted with $21-a-gallon Ralph Lauren interior house paint in such colors as Picket Fence White and Golden Retriever. Much better choices than Ratty Straw Garden Hat Yellow and Maid's Uniform Blue. The slots on the screws that hold on the light-switch plates are all horizontal. If only they had spent as much time designing their marriage as they had this house. They spent more time deciding on the bedroom carpeting than they did on whether or not to have children and how to raise them.

When you look out the window you see twenty or thirty houses just like this one. Each family took the same notes in the middle of the night and had the same discussion over the same kitchen, has the same miserable life. When the neighbors come to visit, they know where everything is, every coffee cup, every carving knife. The houses always have one thing being built—a bedroom, a deck, a security system—because the couple knows, on some level, that when the house is finished they are, too.

---

*H*AVING HEARD MY thoughts on the subject once, maybe twice before, Sue says, "I'm taking it you're not interested in looking at a weekend house with me?"

I gave her The Look. "Like I want to see Henry Winkler's *Hamlet*."

"Fine, Beverly will go with me."

Oh great. Beverly. This is not going to have a happy ending. I always get the impression Beverly's thinking, Sue could have done so much better than this jerk. Beverly, the health food nut. Suddenly all the tumblers fell into place. That must be who talked Sue into quitting cigarettes! Home-wrecking lousy Beverly! Beverly the topper. Anything you said, Beverly could top. You went to a play, she'd seen it the week before with a better cast. You went to a movie, she'd read the book. You mention a restaurant, she'd say how much she liked it "before it got popular." You could say you went over Niagara Falls in a barrel and she'd say she saw you while she was walking a tightrope across it. Well, never mind. When it came to husbands, I think Sue topped her. Besides, whenever I saw her with Bert, all I could think was, Poor bastard, he could have done much better.

---

*Q*UITTING SMOKING. THAT was how it all started. It was as if the nice lapsed Catholic I had married fifteen years ago came home one afternoon and said, "Oh, by the way, honey, while you were out I joined the Wiccans and we'll be moving to Salem in the morning. Be a dear and start packing, would you?"

Let's see, I've been smoking since you could buy a pack of unfiltered Camels for twenty-three cents a pack. You put a quarter in the machine and out came a pack of cigarettes along with two pennies stuck under the cellophane wrapper. It took three or four of my seventh-grade buddies to scrape up a quarter; we fought over those pennies. Yes, let's quit. Why didn't I think of it first?

I SHOULD HAVE thought of it first. Every day there were fewer and fewer places to smoke. Movie theaters that used to have smoking sections were suddenly no-smoking "By Order of the Fire Department." Right. Where was the fire department last year? Has there ever been a big movie-theater fire? Look what happened to airplanes. First they had smoking sections on planes; then you couldn't smoke on the entire plane; a few years later you couldn't even smoke in the terminals. You want to quit smoking? Take a round-trip flight to California.

It is amazing how quickly this all happened. One Friday we lived in a normal world where everyone smoked; the next Monday you started seeing small groups of people standing in front of office buildings—one arm wrapped around their chest to keep themselves from shivering, the other feeding quick hits of a cigarette to their almost-blue lips. Cabs suddenly started posting "Driver Is Allergic to Smoke" signs. Allergic? Will you swell up and get hives if I light up back here? Why don't you just say, "No smoking," instead of *this* horseshit? But I couldn't stop. I wouldn't stop. I loved smoking.

Sue smoked when we both had hair down to our butts and both wore bell-bottoms, Sue smoked when we got married, she smoked at her desk in the garment district. Who was this nonsmoking Sue? Where did she come from? You'd think she'd would have discussed a life-changing decision like this with me before she did it.

"I did discuss it with you. Many times. I've been planning this for months. The problem isn't that I didn't discuss it with you, the problem is that you don't listen."

"Yeah, yeah, I don't listen. You always change the subject. I'm talking about cigarettes, you're talking about listening."

To PROVE THAT she wasn't the only one with willpower, I quit smoking too—in front of her. After a calorie-filled bucket of chicken almond ding takeout, I would make far-fetched excuses to get out of the apartment, to smoke.

"I'm running down to the deli—we're out of pushpins."

"At nine o'clock at night?"

If I used the stairs, I could smoke two or three cigarettes before even getting out of the building. If she wasn't home, I would sit half in and half out the bedroom window, blowing the smoke outside, watching the never-ending parade of gay men cruising up and down Christopher Street.

Half quitting was the worst of all possible worlds. I was cranky and smoking at the same time. Gaining weight. And fooling no one but myself.

Sue wasn't having a good time of it either, but at least she had actually stopped smoking. The thing about quitting cigarettes is that you suddenly have great, honking blocks of free time on your hands. The twenty minutes you used to spend smoking three cigarettes over two cups of coffee are gone. To be filled with what? The breaks at work that always seemed too short when you were a smoker now seem long and empty. You finish lunch and you want to get the check and leave. Linger? Over coffee without cigarettes? I don't think so. Suddenly, walking home seems a better idea than taking the subway. Anything to keep from having time on your hands. And the benefits of not smoking were slow in coming. "Nothing smells better," said Sue, "but a lot of things smell worse." She didn't say it, but I could tell I was one of those things.

Sue needed a project, something to keep her nonsmoking hands busy. She started talking about buying a weekend house.

"Fine. Whatever makes you happy."

Fine? What was I saying? If fine is here, buying a weekend house is way, way, way over there. What's the matter with Manhattan?

"It's not fine at all. You can't find something to keep your hands busy in Manhattan?"

"You have to *buy* dirt in Manhattan. It's kind of hard to have a garden in a place where you have to buy dirt."

"A garden? When you can buy perfectly good flowers on every corner in town?"

"I want to put my hands in some dirt. I want to get out of town on the weekends. I want a place I can relax. And it wouldn't hurt you to get out of town, either."

"You know I get the shakes when we leave Manhattan."

"No, you get the shakes because you drink twenty cups of coffee before noon and go out drinking with Rob Corona every night and go to bed at four in the morning and then go to work at eight and you eat all kinds of crap and you don't get any exercise."

"I quit smoking."

"You smell like an ashtray."

"Do you need anything at the store? I've got to get some Post-it notes."

"I just bought some. Look in my desk."

"I meant Drano. We're totally out."

"No, there's some under the kitchen sink."

"Did I say Drano? I meant avocados."

"You're going to pay four dollars for a deli avocado to sneak a cigarette? Just smoke already. You don't have to pretend to go to the deli."

"What are you talking about? I have quit smoking. Practically. I'm down to a pack a day. I know what you're think-ing—but it *is* quitting. I was smoking *three* packs a day. Of Camels. Unfiltered. Now I'm down to one pack a day of Merit Ultra Lights. Which is the same as quitting. It's proba-bly healthier than quitting. They're made out of lettuce, so I'm getting the extra roughage my lungs need, too.

"Besides, you're trying to change the subject. What do we need a weekend house for? I don't understand that. People in Indianapolis don't have weekend houses. You know why? Because they like the house they have, that's why. People in Omaha don't have weekend houses. They do the smart thing—they buy a house they like and live in it. They don't live in apartments they hate so much that they need to buy an entire other house to get away from the stench of the first one. Why don't we take the money we're going to spend on a second house and buy a better first one? One that we don't have to get away from?"

"Don't you have to run down to the deli? We're running out of bullshit."

BUT I REALLY couldn't go house hunting; I had work to do. Tonight that meant going to a publicity party for Olan Obert, a fashion designer who has just introduced his per-fume—Eau No! A magazine writer's job is never done. There are movie screenings and fashion shows to go to, chichi parties to attend. The pay is so low that we must ac-cept charity from public relations companies. CDs. Books.

Liquor. Press junkets to Hollywood and Cannes. T-shirts. Monogrammed golf balls. Videotapes of upcoming TV shows. Office supplies. Or did I steal those? No, they sent them to me, little memo pads that say "Delano," from hotelier Ian Schrager. Man, if that doesn't want to make me write a story about his trendy hotels, what will? Ballpoint pens with "The Phantom of the Opera" on them. I was going to say it sucked, but that changed my mind. Stacks of press releases come from movie studios and record companies with 8 x 10 glossy stills and color slides of the stars. I take the photos and autograph them to myself with different-colored Sharpie markers—"Jim, Thanks for everything. Your friend, Burt Reynolds." "Jim, I couldn't have done it without you. Tom Hanks." "Jimmy, I'll never have a weekend like that again. Madonna"—and hang them on my office wall. Visitors think I am very well connected. And in a wee small way, I was. With everyone except my wife. I was disconnected from this nonsmoking, weekend-house-buying stranger who had taken over her body.

I thought we knew each other. For twenty years Sue and I had pioneered one pregentrified Manhattan neighborhood after the next. Soho in the mid-seventies, when you had to throw your keys out the window down to friends on the street if they wanted to come up because the building had no buzzers. Raoul's, La Gamelle, Central Falls, Art et Industrie, the Ear Inn, the Broome Street Bar, Le Zinc, Walkmans, Frosty Myers's big blue mural on Broadway and

Houston, and *au* so *courant* boutiques that didn't open till one in the afternoon.

Chelsea in the late seventies, when you had to bribe cab-drivers to take you there, when chalk drawings of nuclear babies and barking dogs started appearing on blacked-out ads on the subway platforms, when the MTA didn't know whether to strip the graffiti off the subways or sell the cars to avant-garde museums in Europe. Two bedrooms, a living room, dining room, and kitchen on Fourteenth and Eighth above a Chinese-Cuban restaurant for six hundred dollars a month. *Sopa del wonton, huevos foo yung,* and a *café con leche* for $2.99.

Thirtieth and Park, when it was full of welfare hotels and hookers, instead of cappuccino bars and two-star restos; Brownies health food restaurant, between Fifteenth and Sixteenth on Fifth; Barnes & Noble before it was a chain. Princess Pamela's Little Kitchen—"Menus? Honey, I ain't got no menus. I got chicken and I got fish. Whatcha gonna have? I got bourbon and I got gin. Whatcha gonna have?" I had the fish and I had the gin. Was it 1976 or 1986? I couldn't tell you.

What year was the year of shoulder pads? There was a time when every item of clothing had to have shoulder pads. T-shirts had shoulder pads. Michael Musto said you could tell how well a nightclub was doing by how many shoulder pads were swept off the dance floor the next morning. I think the record was nine.

The West Village in the eighties, with two gay bars on every block—the Ramrod, Two Potato, the Anvil, the Spike, the Mine Shaft. Our apartment building on Christopher Street had so many gay men living in it, it was nicknamed Leather Flats. It was in 1983 that a spot illustrator at a magazine I worked for died of something his friends called the "gay cancer."

THERE WAS NO such thing as an uneventful subway ride. Today the car is packed with passengers, most holding a copy of the *Post* with the headline "16 People Killed by Crazed Gunman on the LIRR." Did they really need the word "crazed"? As if this could have been the work of a sane gunman.

One of the advertising cards features human toothpick Kate Moss wearing skimpy Calvin Klein underwear. She looks like she's just been freed from Bergen-Belsen. There is a cartoon balloon coming from her mouth, certainly not authorized by Mr. Klein. It says, "Feed me." Other cards hawk one Madame Rosa in English and Spanish, who will cure you of "curses, spells, and bad luck." Madame Rosa is "located in a refined neighborhood," a place in Flatbush that wouldn't know refined if it bit it on the ass. There are ads from Madame Consuelo and Madame Bela and Madame Z offering similar services. It doesn't take many days of subway riding to understand why Madame Rosa advertises there. If you have to take the train to work every day, you *are* cursed. Another ad promises professional "ear repair," with an illustration of a jagged, torn earlobe that looks as if it had had a pierced earring ripped from it with a pair of vise grips. There is a placard for a hemorrhoid specialist: "Call 1-800-DR-TUSCH!"

A neatly dressed mulatto woman holding the hand of a very cute six-year-old boy enters the car at Times Square and starts to speak in a very loud, theatrical voice.

"My name / is Juanita Jones. I am / a poet. I make / my living / reciting poetry. I call / this poem / 'Spring.'

My love cannot be bought,
My love cannot be sold,
My love cannot be put on lay away.
My love cannot be put on a shelf,
My love cannot be put in a bag,
My love is no deposit, no return.
Paper or plastic?

"Thank you. Any donations / will be / gratefully accepted."

AT LEAST SHE was different. The white-robed beggars, the fake nuns, the legless, the armless, the sightless, the deaf handing out cards were all becoming clichés of subway begging. It was starting to take truly creative deformities to make the big money. Besides, the new thing in subway hustling was entertainment. The A train platform at Forty-second Street now featured four Hispanic-looking guys who mimicked Beatles songs with uncanny perfection. Quite a feat considering they spoke only phonetic English and their Ringo drummed on an overturned cardboard box.

SURE, NEW YORK was a sewer, but it was *our* sewer. Living in the worst part of Manhattan was still better than living in the best part of L.A., the best part of Chicago, the best part of Philadelphia (if there is such a thing). Better to rule in bohemian hell than to serve in bourgeois heaven.

Sue and I could walk to a hundred different restaurants from a hundred different countries, see a different pretentious foreign movie every night, go to off-off-Broadway shows whenever we had the extra cash. Face it, if you are bored in Manhattan, it's your own damned fault. We had worn ruts in the sidewalks to our normal hangouts—Sunday brunch at the Sazerac House, *tortellini ai funghi* at Mappamondo, frozen margaritas at Tortilla Flats, *steak frites* after midnight at Florent, window-shopping the fifty different shoe stores on Eighth Street, getting twelve-dollar Guido haircuts at the Astor Place barbershop, browsing at the Strand, watching matinees at the Film Forum, shopping at Turpin-Sanders in SoHo. Sue was going to give this all up for a weekend house?

———

"ℙERFUME—THE LAZY man's way to make a few million dollars," says Rob Corona. "You can always tell how bad a scent is by how many exclamation points come after the name. There's one perfume out there whose entire name *is* an exclamation point. It can repel a wildebeest. How much you wanna bet the only work Olan did on this was sign his name to the licensing contract?"

We are at Olan's spectacular penthouse on East Fifty-second Street. It is a small glass box à la Philip Johnson, set in the center of a wide green lawn atop a thirty-story prewar co-op. There are cut flowers everywhere. Nothing that actually grows in a pot. I'm wondering if the grass is turf, or cut individually like the flowers. He can afford it. There is a 360-degree view of Manhattan the way it should be seen. Looking down. We are so high you can't hear the traffic.

"Sue quit smoking," I confide.

"It's all over town," Rob mocks. "You must be devastated."

"She's broken the smokers' bond. Am I supposed to pre-end it never happened?"

"You can't. You're just a man."

"She thinks I'm overreacting."

"I'm surprised you're still living with her."

"She makes more than I do."

"The bitch!"

"For a gay man, you know a lot about women."

"You're not seriously listening to me, are you?"

"How stupid do I look?"

"Please, don't set yourself up like that. But now that you mention it, those pleats do make you look fat and stupid."

"I *am* fat. Fat is what makes me look fat."

"You could at least try to camouflage it."

ROB IS A food stylist. He makes models of the food they use in TV commercials and magazine ads. It seems a real cheese-burger would last only about ten seconds under the hot camera lights, so they pay him big money for his fabulous faux food. He makes a small fortune, but like every other person in New York, he wants to be fine artist. Good luck.

But he does make me laugh, and as funny people do, we once tried to write together. We started working on the pilot of a sitcom called *Pioneer Fairy.* The opening shot was an aerial view of a wagon train. As the theme song played, the camera slowly panned from the lead wagon to the back, where you would see the chuck wagon with a Cinzano umbrella opened up on the back, in which lived two gay men on their way to found San Francisco. One was the cook, the other was the train's chief scout. Scout always wore pure white deerskin cowboy outfits with lots and lots of fringe and silver, and he was the best shot in the West. In each episode he would save the wagon train by his skill and daring, while his partner, Cookie, would be busy creating new and experimental food—bison Provençale—for the cow-pokes, none of whom realized Scout and Cookie were gay.

Everyone called everyone "partner." "Who's your partner?" was going to be America's catchphrase if this ever got on the air. There was one unmarried woman on the train, the beautiful Belle, and whenever there was a shooting or a knife fight, she would rip off a piece of her low-cut outfit to dress the wound. By the end of every episode she would be half naked.

What network we thought was going to buy this, and in what lifetime, was never discussed, but plotlines, characters we developed in great detail. It sits in a drawer somewhere in Rob's vast loft.

Rob has one of the great deals in Manhattan real estate— a 150-by-50-foot space on West Twenty-sixth Street, rent free. It had belonged to a mildly famous painter who died and left the loft to his cat. Rob was dating the estate's lawyer. So long as the cat lived, Rob lived rent free to take care of it. Rob is on his third look-alike cat, the original being dead some ten years now. Talk about rent control.

The loft is an immense floor-through; not a wall, front to back. To make rooms, Rob would move the dead artist's large canvases around like Japanese screens. He built a bedroom out of *Blue Heart #4, Leftover Red,* and *Blood Blister.* On some paintings, Rob had hung smaller paintings and photographs of his own.

A WOMAN HAILS me from the left. We exchange heartfelt greetings: "Kiss-kiss, touch-touch, love you with a very

special love, don't ever change, stay just the way you are. And I mean that from the bottom of my heart. Ta." She pirouettes away.

"Who?" Corona asks.

"I don't remember her name but she used to work at *How to Lose 10 Pounds by Friday* and went to *Secure and Single*. They shut down after one issue. I think they owe me money. When it folded she became the cosmetics editor at *New Working Mother Woman*."

"Cosmetics editor. It's my dream job."

"I don't know, somehow I picture you in a factory. Big steel-toed shoes, sleeveless T, a hard hat that says, 'Kiss me, I'm gay.'"

I CAN'T GET over this penthouse. This is what Sue and I need. It may be lonely at the top, but my God, they have so much more space! I try not to be jealous but it would be a delightful place to live. Instead of a view of the ugly building next door, or an air shaft, like I have, Olan can see the Manhattan skyline. It's as if we're watching a silent movie, and down below, the red and yellow lights of traffic, the lights from a million windows fading off into the distance.

From here I could walk to work and never set foot in the sticky subway. I could go the whole day without smelling wino urine. I could see the sky. My doorman would take packages for me. My doorman would wait for the cable guy. It's apartment heaven. Life could not possibly get any better than this.

"Santa Maria della Moda, look at that!" Rob points out into the darkness. About two blocks south there is a building two or three stories taller than this one. We can see the edge of another penthouse backlit by the office buildings behind it. It must be three times the size of this one. There are huge shade trees on its terrace—bigger than any trees down on the street. It's hard to tell, but it almost looks like it might be a replica of the Breakers in Newport. So, maybe life can get a little better.

Rob tosses his cigarette over the waist-high safety wall. "I wonder how we get invited there," he says. "Now *that's* a penthouse."

"Yeah, not like this dump. Tell me, aren't you ever happy just being where you are?"

"Me?" he said. "I'm not the one whose wife is out looking for a weekend house. I'm not the one sneaking out of his own apartment to smoke cigarettes. I'm not the one who wants a doorman."

———

SUE AND BEVERLY took a state map and marked a circle three hours from the city up in the Catskills. The Catskills. That sounds vaguely familiar, I just can't place it.

THE TRAVEL SECTION of the Sunday *New York Times* is bursting with must-see places for the city weary: "The Charming Inns of Vermont," "Vacations in the Napa Valley,"

"12 Out-of-the-Way Things to Do in the Poconos," "Heli-Skiing in Jackson Hole," "Avoiding the Herd on Martha's Vineyard," "The Connecticut Not on the Map."

There is nothing quite like it. If it can be gotten to, they print it; if it can be gotten to easily, they do an odd take on it. If it is totally remote—the last thing you would ever do with your vacation dollar—there is a good chance it will be the cover story: "Off the Beaten Track in Gabon," "Seven Days in Socotra," "Secret Sri Lanka," "The Untouristy Side of Kinshasa," "Living with the Yanomamo for Only $300 a Day!"

The ads for travelers are filled with bargains and romance: "4 days, 3 nights in Cozumel," "Las Vegas Bellagio, Airfare Included," "Air France 10-Day Parisian Special!"

But there is one travel destination that you will never, never, never, ever, ever, ever read about in the Travel section in the *New York Times*. It is a place so remote, so uncivilized, so unknown, so dangerous that even their most adventurous travel writers avoid it. That place is upstate New York.

Upstate is to New York City what Canada is to the United States—a great, empty space to the north that most people are quite happy to know nothing about. Its borders are unknown, its rivers impassable, its villages a mystery. Ask anyone in New York City where Binghamton is and if you're lucky you will get a blank stare. If you are not so lucky you will be told with confidence that it is a large manufacturing city in the north of England. These are the same folks that can tell you where to eat in Positano and the best place to stay on Minorca, but they couldn't find Utica on a bet. Ten years ago I couldn't have, either.

CLOSER THAN THREE hours away, real estate was too expensive; farther than that was too far to drive. Sue and Beverly took a week off and went to look at property. At least there is one good thing about the Catskills. It's six hours from the Hamptons.

Sue came back from her house hunt empty handed. She and Beverly spent a week with a real estate agent looking at properties. Each time he showed her something, she told him what was right with it and what was wrong with it. The driveway's too long, it's next door to a mobile home, it's on a main road not a back road, it's too big, it's too expensive.

It's just as well. This is a phase. She'll get over it. I tried to be supportive, but no matter what I said, she wouldn't start smoking again.

Rob was no help. He calls people like Sue and me the "second homeless," poor Manhattanites who have only one house. Oh, the humanities! Won't you please give till it hurts? Let these poor unfortunates get another, larger, more expensive house, preferably in a resort community near a golf course or a beach. Won't you please pay higher taxes so they can buy cheap government flood insurance for their multimillion-dollar homes and so better roads can be built to get them there faster?

• • •

BUT IT WAS too good to be true. A week or so later, Sue's upstate real estate broker called. Come quick. You should look at a piece of property that just came on the market, it's perfect for you. Sue took a day off work, rented a car, and came back with a contract on a house. I need a cigarette.

———

*I*T'S FRIDAY. I should be working on my column, but no, we have to drive upstate to sign the papers on Sue's new weekend house. I want it perfectly clear that it's her house. I had nothing to do with this. I didn't want this house, I've never seen this house. I like staying in New York City on the weekends. I'm just going because I'm a New Age, sensitive guy. And she makes more money than I do. If she wants to throw her own money away on this crap, well, fine. I can be as supportive as the next fool. That doesn't mean I have to be happy about it.

WE'VE BEEN DRIVING through nowhere on a feature-less road called the Quickway at fifty-five miles per hour for what seems like nine hours in a boat of a rental car. A 1987 Status Seeker or something. It's got automatic seat warmers and sunroof. It looks exactly like every other car on the road. I cannot tell them apart. To me there are two kinds of cars, yellow cabs and everything else. My watch says we've been on the road only an hour and a half but that can't be right. It's some kind of space-time continuum. When we get back to Manhattan, Sue and I won't have aged at all, but our friends will all be eighty. Or maybe I have fallen asleep and lost a day.

Finally she pulls off the highway into a town that looks as if the Unabomber were the head of the planning board. A sign says, "Roscoe, New York—Trout Town USA. Only 90 miles from New York City." And a few centuries. I expect Rod Serling to walk into the frame after we pass by, look into the camera, and say, "Jim thinks he's on the way to his wife's new weekend house. Little does he know his life will never be the same as she drives him into the Twilight Zone." If everything suddenly turns black-and-white, I'm making her turn around.

"We're halfway there. The rest of it's on a county road."

"Halfway there? You mean this isn't it?"

"God, no. This is much too close to New York. It's full of city people." No, New York is full of city people, I want to say, but some days I get lucky and don't say everything I think.

"I'M DRY," SUE said, her eyes on the road. "Yesterday I tried 'the color of a dog running away.'" Sue works for a yarn company in the garment district and one of her jobs is to name the colors for each new season. Nothing in the fashion world is ever simply blue or green—how would customers know that it was not something from last season or, God forbid, last year? The name had to scream: Right Now, Today, This Very Moment. Sapphire, emerald, topaz, lapis lazuli. Blueberry, strawberry, grape, tangerine. Rose, magnolia, iris, peony. Bone, heather, teal, aubergine. Concrete, steel, brick, acoustic tile. All had had their run. After ten years, four seasons a year, she was running out of ideas. It was getting hard not to repeat herself.

"I like that."

"I read it in a book. But who's going to buy a blouse with that on it? Can you see the rest of the line? 'The color of a cat deciding to go out,' 'the color of a parakeet going to sleep.'"

"How come you never take any of my suggestions?"

"Mold? Crustacean? Grill brick? Steak tartare? Beer? Great. How about 'the color of me working at McDonald's'? Thanks, but I'm not looking for a *worse* job than I already have."

"Your job is a piece of cake. You sit at a desk all day."

"Thanks. Sometimes you are just so huggable."

"I know what I'm talking about. I've had a lot of bad jobs. I've spent a lot of time thinking about bad jobs. You want to know what the worst job in the world is? The worst job in the world is putting those little rubber bands on lobster claws. That would have to be the worst. What could you possibly get for doing something like that? Minimum wage? And what about benefits? They probably don't even get benefits. I mean, the most money you're ever going to make putting the rubber bands on lobster claws would be if one of them snaps off your little finger. Then they'll give you, like, I don't know, fifteen hundred dollars. *Your* job is only the fifth- or sixth-worst job in the world. How about this for a bad job—backup musician to Yanni? Think about it. You're Yanni's first chair violin. Which means you've really got to be able to play the violin, read music, the whole schmear. You've gone to school, you're some kind of doctor of musicology or whatever, but you're forced to play his crap all night long just to make a living. Sure, you get to see the Acropolis, but it's still a pretty sucky job. I'll bet you the guy doesn't even put it on his résumé. 'Played first violin for Yanni.' Next! I'll tell you a bad job—driving the chase car for a wide load. You don't even get to drive the wide load, you're just the guy in the car behind the wide load that has a big sign on the back of his car that says, 'Caution, Wide Load.' You have to drive across the country going thirty miles an hour. Bor—ring, bor—ring."

"I may not know what the worst job in the world is, but I think I know what the easiest one is."

"I can see where this is going. Sure, I may not *physically* do anything on Wednesday, Thursday, Friday, Saturday, Sunday, or Monday, but I'm always thinking about writing that column. It preys on my mind. It may look like I'm doing absolutely nothing. It may look like I'm playing video games or watching television or reading a book or going to movies and cocktail parties, when I'm really struggling to bring some thought worth printing to the surface. When people ask me how long it takes to write my column, I tell them, 'Forty years.'"

"And they say, 'What a pretentious, lazy jerk you are.'"

"Not *all* of them."

WE DROVE OUT of Roscoe on a rough two-lane state road. Suddenly, there were no cars in front of us or behind us. Forty-five minutes past Roscoe we came over the crest of a hill and three counties spread out before us, a mix of farm and forest, mountains and valleys, and endless ribbons of stone fences. The trees were gaudy chorus lines of yellow, red, orange, and tan. Every now and then you could spot a white farmhouse next to a red barn with silos, odd little outbuildings scattered about. Not a 7-Eleven, not a McDonald's in sight. Where are we and what year is it? If Sue starts using hand signals and begins telling me that she's low on gas ration coupons, I swear I'm jumping out of the car.

This road was not made for dawdling along and admiring the view. It was for work. There were no scenic overlooks carved out of the side of the mountain, no blue-and-gold metal signs telling you that someone you never heard of did something you never knew about right about here in 1809. As we passed close by the hay fields we could see the chunks of flat, blue-gray slate that made the fences, the stone foundations of barns that had burned down or rotted away, the walls of postage-stamp-sized family cemeteries with ten or fifteen worn-out tombstones standing in one section, empty spots thoughtfully left vacant for the generations to come, the generations that moved to the cities years ago and would never take their places; an unhealthy number of red-and-white For Sale signs in front of houses and lots; signs for home businesses, like taxidermy and dog grooming; and many, many trailer homes. The custom seemed to be that the family farm would sit in the center of a cluster of mobile homes. It was as if each child in the family, instead of getting his own room, got his own mobile home. Some of them were no longer mobile, having brick chimneys and roofs added, even whole wings attached, but somehow they still looked like trailers. In front of the fancier ones stood an eight-foot-tall brown bear carved out of a single log with a chain saw. People who couldn't afford chain saw bears went with painted wood duck-shaped whirligigs that spun their wings in the wind. Talk about gilding the lily. Every now and then you could get a glimpse through the trees of the small, rounded, chrome-colored trailers—the kind you'd pull behind a car—sitting alone in the middle of the woods. For hunting, I guessed.

And cows. Countless cows. Brown cows, black cows, black-and-white cows, brown-and-white cows. Beige cows. There were a few horses, every now and then some sheep, but mainly cows.

"Why don't they have them spayed? My God, they're taking over."

• • •

OLD, ABANDONED FARM equipment sat in fields near the edge of the road: machines that sprouted an unseemly array of rusting blades and hooks, each one more dangerous looking than the next. I could only guess what they were for. "That's a double-bladed finger chopper. Oh look there, an International Harvester child impaler. Wow, a John Deere leg remover. There's an old Ford dethumber. Hey, look, you don't see many of them anymore, a rotary eyeball plucker."

"A bank," said Sue, breaking my rhythm.

Sue nodded to a mobile home in the middle of a hay field with a sign that said, "First National Bank of Bob," I'm not kidding. Well, it didn't say "of Bob" but it was in a mobile home.

Bankin' Bob couldn't have been nicer. He even moved most of his lunch to one side of his desk to give us a little working room.

"So," he introduced himself, "you both got jobs?"

"Yes."

"Well, that was quick. Loan approved."

"Would you like to know what they are?"

"Just more to write. I'm not big on forms. If you're lying, well, shame on you."

MINUTES LATER WE were the proud owners of One Oak, a farmhouse I had never seen.

"Doesn't it bother you that our bank is on wheels?" I

asked Sue. "How do you even know it's going to be here next month? What if we've just given a big down payment check to a scam artist? As soon as we leave, he could hook that bank up to a truck, move it into the next county, and rob a few more city slickers."

Sue thought about it for a second and said, "You're an idiot."

SHE IS STILL pissed at me because back in 1978 I told her that Betamax video recorders were never going to drop to under $800 and she should buy one *now*. Till the day she dies, I know this will be the first thing that comes to mind whenever she thinks, *Jim*. It's been over twenty years and she keeps a few unplayable Beta tapes around the house lest anyone forget what a total and complete fool I am when it comes to investment advice. To her it happened yesterday. The sweet things, the cute things, the funny things I do, she never remembers. The gaffes, the missed dinners, the stumbling home drunk, the broken pottery, the coming home at 5 A.M.—she can remember the year and the date, the hour, the minute. Of course, now that I think about it, I was the only one who thought the broken pottery was cute, the stumbling home at 5 A.M. funny.

FROM THE BANK we drove again, turning off the two-lane blacktop to a one-lane, twisting, potholed dirt road, trailing mighty clouds of dust behind us. There was the smell of wood smoke in the blue, crisp air, perfect football weather. It was the first week of October and I was glad I left the lining in my new black gabardine trench coat. It was cold out, much colder than it had been in the city. A dry snowflake whooshed up the windshield.

FROM THE TOP of a rise I could see a large saltbox barn, a small clapboard farmhouse with a smoke-stained cinder-block chimney at the bottom of a postcard-looking valley. A stone fence lay between the barn and the house; a row of sugar maples lined the road, their leaves red and orange. A Martha Stewart starter kit, a Kodak moment.

"Now, that's what you should have bought," I said.

"I did."

THE HOUSE WAS tiny, but compared to our one-bedroom Manhattan apartment it was San Simeon. It had rooms for things we didn't even have drawers for at home. A laundry *room*! A *pantry*! A *basement*! A mud*room*! Guest bedrooms— three of them! At two per room we could have six guests in our house. In Manhattan two guests were a chore. A dining *room*! Two people could stand in the kitchen at the same time and not worry about catching a sexually transmitted disease. Linen closets, broom closets, clothes closets. We had a back door, a basement door, a side door, and a front door. Out the picture window in the living room we could see a small brook that ran down the valley floor, cows grazing, lifting their heads once in a while to consider the new neighbors. We'd been here for ten minutes and not another car had come down the road.

All this for a third of what our tiny Christopher Street apartment had cost. I'd lived in Manhattan so long that I'd forgotten it wasn't unusual to have more than two rooms in most of America, that you didn't have to be Oprah-rich to have a dining room *and* a living room.

THE HOUSE OOZES character—there isn't a square corner or a level floor in the place. Drop a marble on the kitchen floor and you can watch it roll from one end of the house to the other and back again. Like some M. C. Escher drawing, it defies the laws of nature, first rolling uphill into the dining room, then gathering speed as it whips around all four walls of the living room. In one empty room, a strange optical illusion occurs when Sue and I pass each other. It appears that she grows taller while I shrink. The glass in the windows is so old that it ripples and runs as if it had been sliced from a frozen waterfall. Through certain windows it always looks as if it is raining.

A black, cast iron woodstove about the size of an office Xerox machine stands in the corner of the living room. It has a solid cast iron door with two spinning knobs that let you adjust the airflow to the fire, from nothing to a roaring furnace. The real estate agent called it an airtight stove and said with a little practice you can keep a log or two burning slowly all night long. What would it cost to have someone come and remove it?

The house is a museum of every horrible idea in interior design of the past fifteen decades. Contact paper, avocado ovens, wood paneling, kitchen pass-throughs, plastic lighting fixtures, dropped ceilings, aluminum storm windows. The ground-floor bedroom that will be ours is covered in Care Bears wallpaper. "Make it a rainbow day!" repeats one bear, up one wall and down the other.

There is an old outhouse in the backyard that has been turned into a toolshed. A proper moat of mown green grass surrounds the house, and beyond that, hay fields. I guess it's hay. You could say it was rye or barley or soybeans and I'd have to believe you. Do they plant hay, or is it grass they don't mow often enough? Make a note, look into that.

THE VALLEY TWISTS and turns, and the only other house we can see is a bigger farmhouse with its barns and silos and outbuildings a quarter mile down the road. I later learned there are only seventeen houses on Spilt Milk Road, all six miles of it.

OUR BARN IS much bigger than the house. It is painted red. The roof is made of wooden shingles.

"Shakes," Sue says.

"It seems pretty steady to me," I answer, knocking on a hand-hewn beam. "These have got to be ten or twelve inches thick. Look, you can see the tool marks. This thing is ancient."

Daylight knifed through the knotholes and spaces and missing planks on the sides of the barn like a thousand light sabers crisscrossing the dark. It was like being inside a planetarium made with a hatchet and an AK47. A previous owner had been a taxidermist, and unclaimed deer heads and skulls were hung about, as well as a few old farming tools—a yard-long blade with teeth three inches across and three inches deep, some wire, a couple of paint-splattered sawhorses, empty feed bags, old newspapers, worn-out tires, three shaky mismatched chairs, oil cans, a forty-eight-star flag, a set of free weights, and a bench. Thousands of flies were banging themselves into the windows trying to get out.

"I suppose you'll be wanting to turn this into the guest house," came a voice from the door. Sue and I both turn to see a tall, thin, gray-haired woman in a plain woolen jacket, worn jeans, and Wellingtons, carrying what looks to be a walking stick. "I'm your neighbor, Abby Taylor. We live on the next farm." She thumbed to the collection of buildings down the road. We introduced ourselves and asked why we would want to put our guests in the barn.

"Sorry. I thought every flatlander that moves up here turns the barn into a guest house. Still, I was wondering, could you give me a hand? One of the heifers is loose and Al's up on the hill."

Before I can say, "What's a heifer?" Sue says, "Sure, what can we do?"

Abby tells us to grab a stick or something and follow her. Sue gives me the say-one-word-and-you'll-wish-you-married-Lorena-Bobbitt look. I don't say, "What do I look like, lady, Hopalong Cassidy?" but follow them out of the barn.

"YEE—HA!"

"What are you doing?" Abby says, giving me a puzzled look.

"I'm yelling 'Yee—ha' at the cow. Didn't you ever see *Rio Bravo*? John Wayne? Dean Martin?"

"We don't see too many new movies up here. I'm sure she likes the 'yee-ha-ing' and all, but all you have to do is stand here. See that gate in the fence? If you two could just stand on this side of the gate the heifer won't go past you, and with me on the other side, she'll just walk through the gate where she's supposed to be. She'll be on the meat wagon if she gets out again. I got chores to do. I ain't got time for no cows that can't behave."

With our help it took twenty seconds to get the young cow herded, but it would have been impossible to do it alone. Before I could ask what a flatlander was and do people still use the word "chores," Sue caught my elbow and turned me around. Make a note. What's a meat wagon?

"Let's get back to the house."

"Yeah," I say, "it's getting cold out here and herding cattle has given me quite an appetite."

The sun dropped behind the mountain and in its shadow the temperature fell faster than a Richard Branson hot air balloon on a trip around the world. It went from sunny to dark in about three minutes, from brisk to brutal in four. There is an indoor/outdoor thermometer over the kitchen sink. Outside it is thirty-nine degrees. Inside it is thirty-eight degrees.

"I'll start a fire," Sue volunteers.

"No, just turn up the heat. We'll be back in the hotel soon, there's no point in starting a fire."

"What hotel? What are you talking about?"

"Well, where are we staying tonight? Don't tell me we're driving back. I don't think my back can take it. I just want to kick back and watch a little TV. Maybe order in some Chinese."

"We're staying here tonight. And we're staying here tomorrow night, and then we're driving back Sunday night. Then next Friday we'll drive back here and stay until Sunday, and drive back, and then the next Friday . . ."

"Nuh-nuh-nuh-no-no-no no. You can stay up here, but I got places to go, people to screw. You never said anything about staying up here all weekend."

"Remember that discussion we had about you not listening to me? I've been telling you for two weeks what we were going to do."

"I'm sorry. Did you say something?"

Sue had been carefully arranging paper and kindling in the firebox. "Why don't you go out and bring in some wood?"

"Because it's dark out there. And cold."

"We only need a few armfuls."

I buttoned up my coat and walked out the mudroom door. The stars jumped out vast and crisp, some even had different colors—flame blue, faint red. That can't be right, it's a trick of the eye. I could even make out the misty white blur of the Milky Way. There's Orion's belt. The stars were easy to see. The woodshed wasn't. It couldn't be fifteen steps from the back door but I couldn't see it. There it is, dark black against pitch black. Like bad matte work in a seventies sci-fi movie. What's that snorting sound? There's something out here. Something big. Or is that cow out again? Or is it a bull this time? Did Abby say anything about having a bull? If a heifer can get out, why can't a bull get out? If there's a heifer, there had to be a bull, right? No one will believe this—"Columnist Gored to Death on Upstate Farm." Do they have wolves up here? Do they have wolf men? This is eerie. I can hear dogs barking way up the hill. I pick up a piece of wood and cradle it in my arms. I reach for another piece and feel something scurry across my hand, which makes me drop the first piece. Get a grip. One piece, two piece, three pieces, something squishy and sticky, four pieces, something crumbly, five pieces. That should last us a couple of days. Besides, it's all I can lug back to the house. Sue has the kindling going and I drop the logs next to the woodstove.

My beautiful, expensive trench coat is covered with moss, bark, dirt, dry rot, mushrooms, dead bugs, sap, seeds, and some round sticky burrs.

"Two or three more loads like that should get us through the night," she says.

"If not, we can always burn my coat. That should give off some heat."

BEDS WERE THE ONLY FURNITURE in the house; there was not a chair to sit on, not a table on which to put a cup of coffee. There was no coffee. Not that you would want to drink any coffee, because then you would have to use the bathroom. The bathroom combined all the worst features of Appalachian and European plumbing in one convenient spot. Why they brought this toilet indoors one can only guess. Keeping up with the Clampetts, no doubt. I try not to touch anything and hope not to fall through the floorboards while I pee. I wonder which stains in the toilet are from hard water and which are from a bad case of amoebic dysentery. The shower has two bare copper pipes running up the wall over the tub to a garden hose nozzle. There is no pressure; water trickles out in a miserable stream so thin it's a wonder it makes it all the way to the tub. The sink has one handle, *Cold,* and it's mislabeled. It should say *Damn Cold.* Your hands come out clean and numb at the same time. Oh God, why couldn't Sue have bought something in the Hamptons?

SUE PULLED A cooler full of stuff from the trunk of the car. We made sandwiches on the kitchen counter and ate them standing up. There was no television, nothing to sit on and watch it if there were. Sue handed me a bag of several of the new books that I hadn't gotten around to reading. She also brought a stack of CDs I had been meaning to listen to.

"We'll get a boom box tomorrow. You can hear what you've been missing."

"I'm missing television, cigarettes, movies, a phone, New York, and my friends."

"Yes," she said, "your life is a living hell." I went into the bedroom to read. The fire was getting uncomfortably hot.

WE LIE IN bed reading. There are no night tables, no reading lamps, no clicking between infomercials on late-night television. We read by the overhead light. When Sue puts her book down, I get up and hit the switch. She starts to laugh.

"What?"

"Look up."

I look up—there are a thousand stars. One of the kids from one of the families from one of the years before us had stuck up hundreds of little fluorescent stars of different sizes on the tacky acoustic-tiled ceiling. We've had the house thirteen years now; they are still there.

Not once that night did I hear a horn honk, a police siren, the rant of a belligerent drunk, the mad bellow of an EDP. No car-sized boom boxes, no car alarms, no backup beeps, no ambulances, no fire engines, no street fights, no smashing bottles, no garbage truck compactors, no random gunshots. I know because I was up all night. Who can sleep in this unnatural quiet?

Are they *sure* that peace and quiet are good for you? Have there been studies done? Is there scientific proof? Didn't Truman Capote write some book about an isolated farm family slaughtered in their sleep?

"What's the matter?"

"It's too creepy. I can't sleep here. You'll have to sell the place."

———

ONCE IN A great while, out-of-towners would stay with us overnight in Manhattan. In the morning we would always find them standing at the living room window, bleary eyed and tense.

"How can you stand the noise?"

"What noise?"

"My God, we thought it was the end of the world. You're telling me you didn't hear that?"

"Hear what?"

"The helicopters! Tell me you didn't hear the helicopters!"

"What helicopters?"

"There must have been six of them. And ambulances and police cars. Turn on the news, man, quick. Charles Manson must've escaped. And he's on your block."

There is no mention of Charlie Manson's escape to Christopher Street on the television. There is no mention of anything on Christopher Street in the *Post,* the *News,* or the *Times.* The only murders in New York City last night were far away, in places like Queens, the Bronx, and Brooklyn.

WHEN THE FIRST light starts coming through the uncurtained windows of our new bedroom, the silence is broken with an annoying squawking, chirping, singing racket. I get out of bed and look out. There are twenty or thirty birds hopping around on the ground, flitting, moving, jerking, preening, and flying. There is frost on the ground; the indoor/outdoor thermometer says twenty-three degrees. That can't be right. It's only October. Make a note, replace the thermometer.

While Sue slept I dragged the old chairs from the barn into the house. And the two sawhorses. I threw a plank across them and called it a table. If only there were something to put on it. Home Sweet Weekend Home. While I'm up here in Sleepless Hollow spending an exciting cow-filled, furniture-free weekend, I miss the opening of a Greenwich Village boutique that sells novelty condoms, two movie screenings, and a party out on the *Frying Pan,* a restored

Lighthouse boat anchored out in the Hudson. Where are Sue's priorities?

Still, it is picturesque, if you go in for that sort of crap, which I don't. Down the road comes a tractor towing a wagon full of dirt. How rustic. We're living in a cheesy postcard, I remember thinking. As it passes our house the baseball-capped driver waves at me. I wave back through our new dining room window. It must be Abby's husband. What did she say his name was? Albert, Antoine, Al? The tractor disappears past our barn and then we see him out in the hay field. He seems to be driving back and forth for no reason. Soon he goes back up the road the way he came. He waves again, I wave back.

"At least he's friendly," I say to Sue, who has finally rolled out of bed. There are tears rolling down her cheeks. "Oh, come on, let's not get all mushy about it." Since she has really stopped smoking, she smells it before I do. Then my tobacco-deadened nose gets a whiff of what is watering her eyes.

"What is that?" I ask, clamping my hands over my nose and mouth. "Sulfuric acid? Rotting chestnuts on an open fire? The remains of Jimmy Hoffa?"

Waving Al had just covered one of our five acres with a layer of fresh, stinking cow manure.

"How often," I asked, "do you think that happens? Once a week? Once a month? Every day? How long does that smell last? A week? A month? A day? Can't he spread it on his own land? Even then we'd smell it. That can't be sanitary. If we went and spread our manure on his lawn he'd probably hit the roof. We're putting a stop to this right now."

"You're putting a stop to nothing. He's doing what farmers do. While you were yee-ha-ing yesterday Abby asked me if Al could keep haying that field. She even offered to pay. I told her to keep on doing whatever they had been doing before we came. Besides, I'm going to need some of that manure for my garden this spring, so he can dump as much of it on our land as he wants."

"Fine. Make a note, one huge, giant, humongous, industrial strength Airwick. Let's run into town and get the papers and some coffee and see if the smell dies down."

MANY TOWNS IN upstate New York are named after persons and places in Greek and Roman literature: Ithaca, Syracuse, Rome, Utica, Homer, Scipio, Ovid, Macedon, Hannibal, Cato, Elmira, Phoenix, Delphi Falls, Fabius, Troy, Cincinnatus, Pompey, Attica, West Sparta, and Marathon. It speaks to the classical education of the early American boosters who founded these towns. They were starting a new world based on the ideals of the old. Our founders had different goals. Our town is named Walleye.

Downtown Walleye is ten minutes away, five of it on Spilt Milk Road, the other five on the two-lane county highway. We pass maybe six cars on the way.

"Why is everyone waving at us?"

"I don't know. Maybe the tailpipe is dragging or one of the headlights is broken or something."

Sue stops. I get out and walk around the rental car. Every thing seems OK. A car goes by and the driver waves. We wave back, not knowing why.

THERE IS NO weekend crush in Walleye. There is no frenzy for lemongrass or tomatillos at the local farmers' market. There *is* no farmers' market. Just farmers buying their groceries like the rest of America, at the supermarket. There are no second homes that look like they were designed by Frank Gehry or Robert Venturi on their particularly creative days. There are no Land Rovers or BMWs. The vehicle of choice seems to be a Ford pickup or a Chevy Blazer. On the back of the trucks are bumper stickers that read, "No Fat Chicks," "My Student Beat Up Your Honor Student," or "This Is Not an Abandoned Vehicle." Many drivers have named their cars. "L'il Bomber" and "The Duke" are quite popular. There are no Korean delis, no cute boutiques that can get away with selling just one thing, Mrs. Fields cookies or Ben & Jerry's ice cream. No Gap, no Williams-Sonoma, no Barnes & Noble, no theme restaurants owned by the children of celebrities. We can make our own coffee and cookies, thank you very much. Most stores were multibusinesses: Smalley's Video and Septic Tank Cleaning, Henderson's Fine Furniture and Snowmobiles, Cole's Hair Salon and Taxidermy, Satellite Dishes 'n' Floral Wreaths. The only place to eat is the Big Pig

Family Style Restaurant. There's a sign in the window that reads, "Eat Here or We'll Both Starve." There are no cute antique stores with old wooden sleds and hurricane lamps hanging from the ceiling, selling round oak claw-feet tables. No bars with thousands of brands of microbrewery beer, no retro seventies boutiques selling vintage clothes, no Sharper Image selling fancy toys for grown-ups. No reeking-with-atmosphere, crammed-to-the-rafters newsstand where the literati stop by after brunch. There isn't a tuna carpaccio with black-olive *tapénade* on a bed of hand-torn *frisée* within three hours of the place.

THE WALLEYE TOWN square was once on the cover of the *Saturday Evening Post*. In 1951. No, Norman Rockwell didn't paint it, but someone with his nail-the-duck's-feet-to-the-floor, too-good-to-be-true style did, and they got in the redbrick courthouse with its gray slate mansard roof; the you've-seen-one-you've-seen-'em-all Civil War monument; the white, wooden, octagonal bandstand. It looks the same today as it did on that cover, like a set left over from *The Music Man*. The artist left out the three white clapboard churches that frame the other two sides of the square, as well as a post office, decorated by the WPA. The town is two streets deep on each side of Main Street, with rambling old Colonials, square Federals, proud Georgians, and fussy Victorians shaded by big old sugar maples. If you walk more than four blocks north or south you will be trespassing on

someone's farm. No business is open past nine o'clock at
night, and at 10 P.M. the town's single stoplight stops changing from red to green and starts blinking yellow.

A COMMUNITY COLLEGE that looks as if it was designed
by a cabal of the worst Soviet bloc architects vandalizes a
hillside above the town. It saves the town from being too
cute for words. I grew up near Colonial Williamsburg and it
always bothered me that it was so perfect. As if all the
founding fathers painted their houses every year and all of
them were on the neighborhood lawn patrol. Surely, there
must have been a few revolutionaries who let their grass
grow too long, who let their flower borders go all to hell.

On the southern outskirts of town, there is a small strip
mall with a supermarket at one end and an A-Mart at the
other. A Laundromat, a pizza parlor, a beauty salon, and a
drugstore are in between.

"I hear people come all the way from Trout Creek to shop
here," I said.

"And if you embarrass me you can get a ride home with
one of them," Sue warned.

The A-Mart is like a Kmart but not as classy. Everything
is not only off-price, it is off-brand. They have Ralf Loran
shirts, Yugo B. Oss ties, DKYN purses, Lumberland hiking
boots, sheets and towels from the Marty Stewart collection.
The electronic section is packed with unsellable $6.99 CDs
like *The Greatest Public Domain Instrumentals of All Time* by the

Taiwan Symphonic and telephones and portable radios that have been made in countries that have neither phones nor electricity.

I bought their top-of-the-line Zony boom box so we'd have something to listen to when we got back to the farm. Sue filled the cart with other things we needed to make One Oak livable. Spic and Spin, Scrotty paper towels, brooms, mops, Sharman toilet paper, mousetraps, rattraps, glue traps, crawling bug spray, flying bug spray, creeping bug spray, bugs-you-don't-even-know-how-they-get-around spray, a vacuum cleaner, Windox, a dish strainer, sponges, a coffeemaker, and a can opener. Sue had brought a box of old pots and pans with her and some dishes she'd been meaning to give to Goodwill since 1974.

THE NEXT STOP was Agway, the seed and feed store. It was crammed with items needed for life on the working farm. Once you figured out what most of these things did, you didn't want to do them. Bag balm, swine brushes, ear tags, barn shovels, giant bovine syringes, hoof trimmers, prebaited Japanese beetle traps, flypaper, beaver traps, wormers, seed corn, seed potatoes, hominy meal, calf scales, electric fence batteries, barbed wire, gloves, thermal-quilted flannel shirts, and muck boots.

Sue picked up a wheelbarrow, a hoe, a couple of rakes, and a pair of pruning shears. As we waited to check out I was embarrassed by how hopelessly overdressed we were. I was wearing a shirt that actually had a collar and sleeves, pants that didn't have any holes or bleach stains on them, and shoes that weren't caked with mud and cow shit. I felt like I was dressed for the prom and Sue was my date. The guy in front of us was wearing jeans three sizes too big that look like something Jackson Pollock would have worn if he had had a Brown Period. Over this was a T-shirt the color of well-done meat loaf and a stiff brown Carhartt canvas jacket. The guy seemed to be covered head to toe with a light coating of confectioner's sugar. The clerk wore a cleaner version of the same uniform. They were talking some foreign language.

"Half the herd's got the scours, the other half is giving underweight. I had two freshen last night and we lost one calf. The butterfat's way down. The bulk truck took out a piece of my driveway last week and the unloader broke on the big silo. The whitewasher came this morning, so that killed the whole of yesterday getting everything wrapped for that. And some flatlander is suing me for spreading manure because he don't like the way it smells. Like *I* do! What does he expect me to do with it? Leave it in the barn?"

It was becoming clear to me that this guy should be the one with a weekend house; *he* should be the one taking time off. He did more work this morning than I did last week. What did I need to relax from? Too many hors d'oeuvres?

• • •

59

NOWHERE CAN WE find the *Times,* much less the *Post,* the *News,* or *Newsday.* The guy at the Agway wasn't sure, but he said we should try the Happy Camper.

"There's always some flatlanders in there buying something weird. Maybe they got what you want."

"WE'RE IN A store that sells barbed wire and bag balm and he thinks someone else's stuff is weird?" I say as Sue and I load stuff in the car. She makes a shushing noise.

But the Agway guy is right. The Happy Camper is weird. The place is a Deerfield Village of late-sixties culture. It's like visiting the Amish, but instead of living without electricity, they live without Western food and medicine. The walls are lined with Moosewood cookbooks, herbal teas, bulk bins of wild rice, arborio rice, brown rice, polenta, groats, and pignolis. Echinacea extract, hawthorn flowers, CoQ-10, DHEA, cat's-claw, grape seed extract, bee pollen, chromium picolinate, ginseng, blessed thistle, chamomile flowers, lecithin, fish oil, saw palmetto, melatonin, kelp, kavakava, colon cleaners, St. John's wort. And this is just the pet section. There is a sign in the front door that says, "Buy One Shark Cartilage, Get One Free."

Notes on the bulletin board announce the weekly schedule of alternative activities. Monday is the Get-A-Grip Coping Center; Tuesday night is Yogercise; Wednesdays, the Angry White Women Who Run with the Wolves; Thursday is Chanting and How to Make Cheese from Your Own

Goats; and Friday is Become a Licensed Grief Counselor in Your Spare Time at Night Night.

Saturday morning is apparently Let Your Obnoxious Children Run Wild and Do Whatever They Want Day.

"Earthshoe," pleads one mom, "how many times have I told you not to stick your hands in the kasha? Deepak, focus your inner energy or I'll make you go sit in the car!" There is a large display of a new book by a local author: *High Colonics from Your Inner Angels.*

Surely this place would sell the *Times.*

"You're the second person to ask that. The flatlander who bought the Marshall place asked a few times, but nothing came of it. I think they live in a yurt up on Federal Hill now. Sorry, but you have to go to Endicott to get the *Times.*"

"Is that far?"

"Nah, maybe an hour."

WE HEADED BACK to the farm with everything but the newspapers. Where Spilt Milk Road meets the county road there is one of those old-fashioned gas stations, the kind that looks like an old house but the second floor makes a porte cochere for the two gas pumps. Boody's Gas 'n' Go. We pulled up and an elderly man came out and filled the tank. I followed him in and he rang up the sale.

"With the paper, that'll be fifteen dollars and forty cents."

"What paper?"

"Aren't you the one who wants the *Times?*" He reaches under the counter and slaps down the paper. My name is written in pencil on the top.

I introduce myself. "We bought the Henderson place," I said.

"And paid about twenty-two thousand dollars too much for it, I hear."

"You'd be Mr. Boody?"

"Speaking."

"So how did you know I'd be here for the *New York Times?*"

"Anybody that'd pay that much for a falling-down farm has got to be from New York City, and people from the city always want the *Times*. I suppose you'll be turning the barn into a guest house. I may as well start ordering the wallpaper now."

"Thanks, but if there's one thing we won't be doing, it's turning the barn into a guest house."

He made a little we'll-see-about-that humming noise and pushed the paper toward me across the counter, ending the discussion.

WHILE SUE SET mousetraps and sprayed for bugs and cleaned, I set up the Zony boom box and started tuning in stations. Where is NPR? Where is WFAN? Where is twenty-two minutes we'll give you the world? With all my coaxing the only thing I could get was one weak AM station playing some kind of scratchy hillbilly music. It was one of those atmospheric tricks, like getting WLS on the car radio late at night in the middle of the Great Dismal Swamp. Sunspots or something. I threw the Zony back in its box and got Sue to take me back to the A-Mart. She had to drive; my license had expired twenty years ago. The clerk took it out of the box, plugged it in, and tuned in the same fuzzy country station I had gotten.

"See, that's all it gets."

"Mister, it works fine."

"Oh, sure, it gets *that* station, now try and get another one."

"There *is* only one station. The best country music you'll ever hear. It goes off the air at sunset, so don't think there's something wrong with the radio when it gets dark."

"You mean I just spent a hundred and seventy-nine dollars on a radio that can only get one station?"

"Oh, it can get more than one station. Just not here."

We took it home and put it up on the sawhorse table just in time to listen to the scratchy noon news.

That was the Artificial Inseminators with "I Got Up to Pee and You Were Gone," on G-100, WGOD, God's Country radio in the Catskills, bringing you the best country music in the tricounty, artesian well region. And now, The News at Noon with Brian McCovey.

First, the national news. Congress once again did nothing to help the small family dairy farmers.

Now for the local news. Walleye sheriff's office reports a one-car accident on Route 10. Eloise Limestone, eighty-two, of Gilboa, driving a '71 Dodge, swerved to miss a deer and left the roadway. She was taken to O'Malley Hospital for observation and ticketed for driving at an unsafe speed.

Miles Kitson, fifty-four, of East Meridale, was pinned under his tractor for several hours yesterday when it rolled several feet after he got off to unclog the manure spreader. His wife, Abigail, went looking for him when he failed to show up for supper. He said he had been yelling for several hours, but the noise of the tractor drowned him out. He is in O'Malley Hospital overnight for observation.

Rangold Kelly, thirty-one, of Bovina Center, received minor injuries yesterday when a bull attacked him in the high field behind his sugar house. Kelly was treated and released from O'Malley Hospital for minor scrapes and bruises. The bull was taken to Stanley's Meat Packing. There will be a beef barbecue at the Rangold Kelly farm this afternoon for neighbors and friends.

The Walleye town council voted down the proposal to let a McDonald's open in downtown Walleye. Mayor Almay Almerson, owner of the Big Pig Family Style Restaurant, said, "The last thing this town needs is a tacky junk food joint on every corner. One is enough."

The Walleye boys' varsity football will play Schenevus this afternoon, its first game under new coach Norman Paulikowski, who replaced the outgoing Kenny Almerson. Principal Wilson told G-100 News that "Coach Almerson can apply for his job back after his stay at the work farm, but don't quote me."

There will be a spaghetti supper tonight sponsored by the ladies' auxiliary at the Round Barn in Halcottsville. Proceeds to benefit the Coach Almerson Defense Fund. If you need more information, call Almay Almerson at three-seven-oh-four.

There were three fire calls last night, one on Old Dirt Road in Hopkins to put out a brushfire and two separate incidents at the Trout Creek residence of Norman Paulikowski, the new Walleye football coach. One involved a flaming paper bag filled with an unknown substance found on his front steps, and a few hours later much of his collection of lawn whirligigs was found ablaze. Arson is suspected.

The Catskill County Democrats will meet tonight in the potting shed behind Velma Whitehall's house. The county Republicans will meet, as usual, at the high school football field.

In today's almanac, the sun will rise today at nine thirty-two A.M. and set at four fourteen this afternoon; the moon is in its first quarter.

It was two hundred and thirty-six years ago today that Horatio Almerson founded Walleye by planting a flag in what is now the town square and saying, "Those damn Dutch, they make me sick!"

And now a few words from our sponsors. There'll be a sale today through Sunday on specialty manure spreaders at Paulikowski's Farm and Garden Equipment.

Tired of balky, unreliable, old-fashioned manure spreaders? Tired of having to climb down in minus-twenty-degree weather to unclog frozen spreader blades? Isn't it time that you moved up to a Specialty manure spreader? It comes with our patented no-freeze paddles and our safety screen, which eliminates accidental drownings so common with other spreaders. Remember, it's the one spreader to have if you're spreading two kinds of manure.

Dining out tonight? Why not try the Big Pig Family Style Restaurant? If you can find bigger portions anywhere, go there. Try our famous double-pounder, two pounds of ground beef on a one-pound bun. Eat two, and the third one's free. And don't forget, we serve our five-egg omelets all day long. Come and see why there's always a line to get into the Big Pig Family Style Restaurant, the home of deep-fat-fried bacon. Say hi to Chef Bob, the only area chef trained by the U.S. Navy. Kids love his tattoos. That's the Big Pig Family Style Restaurant on Main Street, next to Smalley's Video and Septic Tank Cleaning. With even more tables now that we've eighty-sixed the salad bar. Ask about our Big Pig party platters for your next wedding.

You're listening to God's Country, WGOD, one hundred watts of pulsating power from sunrise to sunset every broadcast day. And now the weather. Snow flurries this morning, followed by sleet and freezing rain this afternoon. Some sun around noon. Dropping temperatures through the night, with accumulations of snow from six to eight inches. The long range forecast: Colder than normal, more snow. Colder in the valleys.

And now back to the music with this week's number four record, the Saddle Blankets with "No Ma'am Is an Island."

We had stumbled into the *Lost Horizon* of media. In the coming years we would learn from Brian McCovey that H. Ross Parrot would be running for president, that Susan

Lucky had gotten her sixteenth Emmy Award nomination without winning, and that Joe Pesky's performance in *Goodfellas* had been nominated for an Oscar. If Brian has the least suspicion that these names are pronounced quite differently in the rest of the country, he never lets on. Perhaps he thinks they're talking about someone else? Wow, what a coincidence, a billionaire named H. Ross Perot and one named H. Ross Parrot both running for the presidency! And both pulling out of the race! What are the chances? I can't wait to hear the results of the Winter Olympics with Oksana Baiul and Picabo Street.

At nine in the morning they play three songs in a row and listeners can win prizes if they can tell the DJ what the three songs have in common. One day each song will be about a truck driver, or all three might have been written by Hank Williams. One morning a caller was absolutely positive she had won the prize. When asked what the three country tunes had in common, her best guess, on live radio, was, "All three songs were full of clichés?"

WE TOOK A walk around the property.

"Do you think that fence is electric?"

"Why don't you grab it and find out?"

"Look at all that poison ivy."

"That's a raspberry bush."

"How does that go? 'Leaves of two, screw you.'"

"'Leaves of three, let it be.'"

"So this is poison ivy."

"That's not poison ivy, it's wild cucumber."

"OK, Little Miss Know-it-all, smarty-pants, tell me this isn't poison ivy. See, it's got three leaves."

"And some red berries. You just pulled up some ginseng. It's illegal to pull it out when it's that small."

"Look, mushrooms. We could be eating off the land tonight."

"Which ones do you want, the death caps or the destroying angels?"

"Oh, just whatever you usually put in your squirrel and possum stew."

"Ha ha ha."

"I can see where Mother Nature comes down on the spanking issue."

"Yes, she's very strict."

"This looks like it came from Mars."

"It's plain old milkweed."

"How can you remember all these names?"

"Break open the stem."

"Yech. It's all milky. Really, where did you learn all this stuff?"

"I don't know. I just pay attention."

"Like I don't?"

"You are the least anal person I know."

"You're just saying that."

"No, I mean it."

"Well, thanks. I don't know what to say."

"Say you'll stop standing in the poison ivy."

WHEN WE WOKE up Sunday morning there were four deer grazing right outside the kitchen window. Two tiny, spotted fawns and two does. Sue and I watched them for twenty minutes as we had our coffee. Slowly they grazed past the woodshed toward the apple trees. They were so close you could see the individual hairs, the drool on their lips. Now, there's something you don't see in the city. They turned and ran when someone drove by in a muffler-free pickup.

SUE TOOK MEASUREMENTS, cleaned, pried, inspected, and probed the house all day. Her hands were busy, she was happy. I read a book without the distraction of a television or a radio. It was time to drive back to the real world. The weather was nicer than it had been all weekend. It was the beginning of what Sue calls the Sunday-night rule. No matter how miserable the weather's been all weekend—rain coming down sideways, sleet, snow, wind, fog—when it's time to pile into the car for the long ride home, the clouds will part, the wind will stop, the sun will shine.

We stopped by the Big Pig Family Restaurant for a quick meal before heading back. At five feet eleven inches, 215 pounds, I still have the body of a teenager. A big, fat, out-of-shape teenager. In the Pig, I feel positively svelte. We have stepped into a Botero *tableau vivant,* or perhaps it is a Duane Hanson sculpture festival. The diners have all been stuffed from the same sausage machine, all with the same gray mottled meat. They share a roundness—round fingers, round arms, round faces—and a bizarre taste in clothes. The men are wearing puffy thermal vests, flannel shirts, and worn-out jeans with wide leather belts. The women wear pink or light blue sweatshirts with designs embroidered on them. The coats on the backs of the chairs are functional, not fashionable; all hoods and zippers and Velcro. It would have to get mighty damn cold before I'd get caught wearing something like that, I said to myself.

"Hey, ain't you the ones who bought the Henderson place?" the hostess greets us. "I think I'm speaking for the whole town when I say thank you. They sure needed the extra money. Him needing that new glass eye and all. Bob at the bank said you might be coming by. He said, 'Ruth Ann, you be nice to those people, they *both* got jobs.' Come sit right here. Something to drink, hon?"

Besides the five-egg omelets and the double-pounder with cheese, the Big Pig's specialty was barbecue pork. Anything that wasn't barbecue pork came with barbecue pork. Barbecue pork was used the way vegetables were used in lesser establishments: "Three eggs, stack of buttermilk pancakes, sausage, and BBQ pork." "Chicken-fried steak, dinner roll, and BBQ pork." "Deep fat fried pork chops with BBQ pork."

"What are you having?" Sue asks.

"I don't know. I'm thinking maybe—barbecue pork?"

"Does that come with barbecue pork?"

"I don't know, *hon*. Or do you prefer to be called 'toots'?"

"Just spreading the joy, aren't you?"

"I'm loving this," I told her. "You paid an extra twenty-two grand for a house that the Joads wouldn't live in and you're snapping at me? I'm on your side. I can't wait to spend our weekends up here churning our own butter and slaughtering our own cows. That reminds me, the next time you're at Bergdorf's, could you pick me up a pair of overalls?"

Ruth Ann delivers our order.

"Excuse me," Sue says, "I got somebody's hamburgers and pancakes. I wanted sausage and pancakes."

"That *is* sausage, hon." Ruth Ann wrinkles her eyebrows at me. I make the universal I'm-with-a-crazy-person, wide-eyed facial gesture and shrug my shoulders.

The hamburger-sized patties on Sue's platter are so big they hang over the edge of the plate. Sue forks into a patty and announces that it is indeed sausage.

"How can they sell this for $2.99?" she asks. "They have to be losing money. It's simply not possible."

"They get a volume discount. And they pass the savings along to you, the pig-consuming customer."

THERE ARE TWO women sitting behind us who either don't know that their voices carry or don't care. While Sue and I eat, it becomes obvious that they are talking about a city couple who have a second home up here.

"They think they're the Waltons. I wouldn't be a bit surprised if they name their kids John Boy and Billy Bob. You know what they got in their kitchen? A G.D. brick oven! ''Cause that's the only real way to make a bread,' she told Charlie when he was hooking up the propane. Well, you could go to the grocery store and buy some, I told him, like everyone else in town, but I guess that never occurred to her. Listen to this, they got a thing to dry their lettuce. Why on earth would you want dry lettuce? They got all this furniture they call 'country style' that he ain't never seen the like of—chairs made out of sticks and twigs, and tables with cracking, peeling paint; pictures that are so old they've turned brown. I lived in the country all my G.D. life and I don't have any of that junk. Why don't she go to Sears like the rest of us? What would she call the stuff in my house? City furniture?"

"Peggy over at the phone company said they put in three lines. One for him, one for her, and one for the computer. Can you imagine? Three phone lines for one house? There's only two lines going into the county jail! Joan at the Shop 'n' Save says that when she shops she never uses coupons, not even the ones in the store flyer. And she buys the weirdest stuff. Whipping cream. Hasn't the poor child ever heard of Cool Whip? Egg Beaters. Half the county can sell you fresh eggs and she's buying fake ones at five times the price. Last week she bought an avocado. Now, what's she going to do with that, I'd like to know? You just plain feel sorry for the poor husband. What does he eat? If I tried to serve Harry an avocado, well, I don't want to think about it. Doesn't the silly goose know how to cook?"

AS THE FOLKS around us finish their meals, they stop by our table.

"We heard what you did for the Hendersons," said one couple in their thirties with five kids that appeared to be six months apart in ages, if such a thing were possible. The pregnant wife said, "We can't thank you enough. Don's my cousin and he really needed the money." The husband chipped in, "I work over to the power company and if you ever need anything ask for John. This is Peggy. She works up to the phone company. And good luck with the septic system."

An elderly woman stops by. "That was so nice what you did. The Hendersons deserve a break after what they've been through. I'm Mrs. Elkins and my son Tom runs the backhoe for Smalley's Video and Septic, so you'll be meeting him soon enough. We talked about it last week at the card game and decided you were either G.D. fools or very nice, and you seem very nice. Eat that, dear. It's a well-know fact that pork is good for you. Look at me, hon, I'm eighty-nine and I can still spit further than anyone here. Stop by the house sometime, we'll have tea. Well, not till spring. I'll be in Tempe till April."

Much to our embarrassment, the tribute to the Mullen Foundation continued. The cashier at the grocery store, who is married to the man who fixes oil furnaces, said hello. Her sister is the volunteer fire department dispatcher and his cousin runs the landfill. His half brother works for the county Department of Roads, which is in charge of plowing Spilt Milk Road in the winter. In the summer he runs the golf cart rentals at the local country club.

"If they ever write a book about this place," I told Sue, "it's going to be called *One Degree of Separation.*"

Sue had hardly made a dent in her sausage. I asked Ruth Ann if we could get a doggy bag. I didn't want it to get around that we were the kind of people who threw away perfectly good food.

IF THE DRIVE up was tedious, the drive back was numbing. In the dark there were no distractions. I was dying for a cigarette. I can't very well run out of the car and say I have to buy some vacuum cleaner bags, Sue would be sure to notice. The food from the Big Pig is being pulled relentlessly toward the center of the earth and it's taking me with it. The headlights of the approaching cars hurt my eyes.

"So go to sleep."

"You know I can't sleep in a car," I told her. That's the last thing I remember until I woke up in the Lincoln Tunnel. Civilization at last.

By the time we returned the rental car and took a cab

home it was almost 2 A.M. As we stepped off the elevator on our floor we heard some horrific screaming. At the opposite end of the hallway from our apartment a small, brown-haired, drunken man was banging on an apartment door over and over, screaming, "David, you can't lock me out, it's *my* apartment!" That night I slept like a baby.

THERE IS A message on the machine from my editor. "Where is my copy? It was supposed to be here Friday. You are the slowest writer I've ever worked with. You're like Stephen King in reverse." Fine, OK, now it's time to pound those keys. This shouldn't take long. I stare at the blank screen. Sue has left for the sixth-worst job in the world. There is an earth-rattling bang. Wait, wait, here comes a thought, we're nearing a complete opening sentence. Bang! Nope, lost it. Bang! What the hell is going on out there? I look out the window. Across the street, two guys renovating a building are tossing bricks, one at a time, into an empty Dumpster four floors below. They are enjoying the noise it makes, the hideous clang of the world's biggest cracked bell.

"How can I work with all this noise?" I ask Rob on the phone.

"Don't be such a big baby whiner. You're the one with the weekend house, not me. I'm the one that had to stay in town, remember? I'm the one that should be complaining. You don't know from problems. I'm in the D'Agostino yesterday. I have a frozen pizza and a diet soda. I'm standing there, I'm the fourth person in line, the pizza is starting to melt. The first person gets through almost without a hitch, but things grind to a halt while they get more paper bags. Who knew all these people coming to the supermarket to-day would want bags? Sure, they needed them yesterday and the day before and every day since they opened, but who knew they were going to need them today? The bags finally arrive. The second guy in line almost gets through with no problem until it came to the funny lettuce. We had to wait while they get a price check on the funny lettuce. Is this Boston, or romaine? The cashier knew all the prices for the next person, but then the register ran out of tape. She had never changed the tape before. My pizza is starting to sag. Ring, ring, ring, ka-ching, there are no quarters. The store manager has to get quarters out of the safe. God for-bid there are too many quarters in the drawer—it's the first thing the robbers ask for, all their quarters. It is some kind of law of nature. The shortest line takes the longest to check out of. I look to see if there is a faster way out. The line next to me is not moving at all. The question that is holding everybody up booms out over the store's PA system. 'Are frozen crab legs "meat" or "deli"?' Instead of having a ten-items-or-less lane, they should have an I'm-willing-to-pay-double-to-get-the-hell-out-of-here lane. That would really move things along."

"I was afraid this call was going to be a waste of time."

"I'm sorry, I can't hear you with all that banging. Talk to you later."

To make the weekly drive to the farm, we bought a car, our first in twenty years. "Who needs a car in the city?" we would always tell our non–New York relatives. "You take a cab, you take the train. Besides, where are you gonna park? On the street? You'd be crazy to have a car here."

But now we had to have one. Sue got a ten-year-old Subaru wagon the color of a dog running away, with only 150,000 miles on it. The big selling point to her was that it had four-wheel drive.

"You don't even know what that means, do you?"

I wasn't going to let her make a fool out of me. "I know it's a hell of a lot better than three-wheel drive," I answered. Make a note, find out what four-wheel drive is.

Once we had the car, we had to find someplace to park. That wasn't going to be a problem because there's a parking garage in the basement of our apartment building. We could park the car down there and get on the elevator to our apartment without having to drive around looking for a spot on the street. We wouldn't have to unload the car in the rain; we wouldn't have to worry about someone breaking into the car while we had our backs turned for five seconds. All we had to do is sign up for a basement parking spot.

"Thank you, Mr. Mullen," said the woman at the building manager's office. "We'll put your name on the waiting list and you should have a parking spot in three or four years."

"Three or four years?"

"I know, everyone thinks it will take forever and it really doesn't. Of course, there's no guarantee that it will still only be three hundred and fifty dollars a month in three years. Like the maintenance, it keeps going up."

Where do we park the stupid car for the next three or four stupid years? Every parking garage I ask in Greenwich Village laughs. If I can afford them, they're full; if they have vacancies, I can't afford them. Finally I found a place that we can afford *and* has the space. It was only a $6 cab ride away from our apartment, in a warehouse neighborhood over by the Twenty-third Street piers.

It's not like parking in the basement, but it'll do. We'll come back Sunday night, park the car, catch a cab, and be home in a matter of minutes.

WE DROVE TO the farm that next Friday night, lit a fire, and fell into bed. I had pleasant dreams of thousands of Care Bears being slaughtered by a Terminatorlike robot.

On Saturday I went to rent a post office box in town: $44.

"Let me ask you something," I questioned the clerk. "If I didn't have a post office box, you guys would deliver mail to my house, wouldn't you?"

He looked up from sorting a stack of Home Shopping Network and QVC boxes. "Yeah, sure. Do you want us to deliver to your house?"

"No, but if you did, it's free, right?"

"Right. RFD. Rural Free Delivery."

"So, explain this to me. If I drive my car all the way into town to the post office and pick up my mail from my box, it costs me forty-four dollars a year. If you guys take your car and drive all the way out to my farm with the mail, it's free. Shouldn't it be the other way around?"

The guy thought for a second, shrugged, and threw up his hands and went back to work. I thought he said something like, "Flatlander!"

THERE WAS A movie we wanted to see playing in Oneonta, thirty minutes away. At first I thought, Thirty minutes to go see a movie? Then I realized I've spent that long in the back of a cab plenty of times going from Greenwich Village to the 68th Street Playhouse. It was a film we couldn't get into in Manhattan; there were lines around the block. We drove to the little mall and walked right in. No lines, no crowd; the tickets were $4 a person.

After the movie we bought some supplies in the mall. Sue sent me off with one load to put it in our new car while she kept shopping. We'd rendezvous at the bookstore in five minutes. Half an hour later I came back, bags still in hand, to tell her the sad news that our car had been stolen.

"You wouldn't expect that in a small town like this, but I went to where we parked it and then I looked all over the lot, but it's gone. Let's call the police."

Sue marched out into the lot, unlocked the beige Subaru

wagon that was right where she had parked it, and threw the bags inside.

"It doesn't look like they did any damage," I said.

"You're an idiot," she replied.

I WAKE UP as Sue pulls into the parking lot I had found. It's 1 A.M., the wind is blowing cold across the Hudson. There are little wind devils whipping up the trash in the gutters. All we have to do is collect our stuff, hail a cab, and go home. But where are all the cabs? They were everywhere when I rented the spot. On a Wednesday afternoon. The fenced-in lot at Tenth Avenue and Twenty-first Street that was thick with uptown traffic and cruising taxis in the daytime was deserted at night—an industrial park surrounded by threatening-looking housing projects. We are in the middle of nowhere with L. L. Bean canvas bags full of the crap we couldn't live without for two days, trying to wave down a cab in the freezing wind. After a half hour or so of anxious waiting—what will come first, a gang of gun-wielding street toughs, or a cab?—we finally flag down a taxi. Obviously it is the driver's first day or he wouldn't be in this neighborhood in the middle of the night. While we have been waiting, four or five other couples in the same situation have driven into the lot and come out laden down with L. L. Bean canvas weekend bags with their distinctive primary color strips identical to ours. We are all waving at the same cab.

"The slimy, scummy bastards! We were here first. Can

you believe the cheek of some people? I've got to get up in the morning!" It was as if we had never gone away. We got home about 2 A.M. The elevator is on the fritz. There is no hot water. After a weekend in the country we're not more relaxed, we're tenser.

———

"*S*o how is Green Acres? Or is it Mr. Blandings' Dream House?" asks Rob Corona.

"Thanks for stereotyping us in the least creative way possible."

He makes a get-used-to-it shrug. We are having the Thursday-night cassoulet at Quatorze on, naturally, Fourteenth Street. "You know what's going to happen, don't you?" Rob says, draining a deep ruby, gin-filled Negroni. "You'll be outta here in five years. Everyone I know who buys a weekend house moves out of Manhattan within five years." He signals the waiter for another round.

"Not live in Manhattan? Please. We love it here. Life is just a cab away. It may be a filthy, disgusting toilet full of perverts, but life without the Angelika Theatre? Without the Film Forum?"

"Not to mention the Knicks, the Rangers, the Yankees, the Mets, Madison Square Garden, and the U.S. Open," Sue adds.

"Miss openings at P.S. 1, Mary Boone, and the DIA Foundation? I don't think so. There's the Met and MOMA, and Dean & Deluca. There are no Balducci's upstate, no Jefferson Market, no Citarella, no Afghan food, no Mappamondo Due, no Coffee Shop, no Union Square farmers' market, no movie screenings, no shushing people whose watch alarms go off during the second act."

How could he even think such thoughts? We are so New York that it's hard to talk to people who don't live in Manhattan. We'd visit relatives out of town and be shocked to find they didn't know who Isaac Mizrahi was, they didn't know that conch carpaccio from St. Kitts–Nevis was going to be the next big thing in food, they weren't all atwitter that Wendy Wasserstein has a new play opening next week. They hadn't read about Pina Bausch in *W.* They hadn't read what Hal Rubenstein said about the food at Moomba in *New York* magazine.

"Why would anyone live anywhere else?"

———

"*IT'S LIKE THEY'RE* in bed with us!" Sue screams. Two drag queens are going at it three floors below on Christopher Street. It is 3 A.M. on an unseasonably hot Wednesday night. Sue has an early-morning meeting. "Where is a vat of boiling oil when you need it?" Everyone told us not to buy this apartment.

"Christopher Street!" they would say. "You've got to be kidding. It's the center of the gay universe." And that was from Rob and his friends. "Oh, come on," we said. "How bad can it be?" But we investigated. We went down on a Tuesday afternoon. We went on a Friday night. A Saturday night. A Thursday morning. It looks just like any other street in Greenwich Village. It was certainly no gayer than any other place in Manhattan. And the price was right. Everything else was at least $50,000 more and not as roomy. This place had an eat-in kitchen, for God's sake. If you ate standing up. On one leg. It had a river view if you stood in the corner of the living room and flattened your cheek against the window. Against everyone's advice, we bought it. On February 7 we moved in. The first day the temperature went above sixty that year was March 2. Sue came home from work and said, "What's going on out there? A street festival?"

That's when we found out that any day the temperature was above sixty, gay men—the clones, the leather boys, the drag queens, the gym rats, the Puerto Rican teenagers who weren't welcome in their own homes—would swim up Christopher Street to spawn. At night there would be great raucous parties out on abandoned Pier 38 that would start at midnight. One evening a fourteen-year-old transvestite took exception to a remark by one of his peers. He took out a pair of scissors and stabbed his rival in the heart. Christopher Street's reputation, we learned, reached way beyond New York. Gay tourists from all over the world would make pilgrimages to our block. It was not uncommon on a hot summer day to see two men dressed from head to toe in black leather—cap, vest, pants, and heavy biker boots—walk down the street conversing in German or Italian. One day I rode the elevator up to my apartment with a gentleman wearing black leather chaps but no pants. His bare, hairy ass was hanging out for all to see. And to think I used to worry that I might leave the house with my *fly* open.

Halloween was not to be believed. The yearly ad hoc parade that attracted millions of sightseers ended on our block. If you carried a drink, a soda, a shopping bag, or a half-eaten piece of pizza, Halloween law decreed you must drop it on the street in front of our apartment before going home. The city would send bulldozers down the street the next morning to clear away the debris.

New York may be the city that never sleeps, but it's also the city that never wakes up. One Sunday morning, before we started going away for the weekends, I went to get the papers about six o'clock. Christopher Street was deserted, the sidewalks empty, no traffic whatsoever. At the corner, in the middle of the lane, as if waiting for the light to change, was a burned-out sedan, all four tires flat, every window broken, the upholstery a melted, misshapen mass of plastic, the dashboard melted like a Dalí painting. No police, no firemen, no emergency services, no bystanders, no victims. I went to get my papers. When I came back, five minutes later, it was gone.

. . .

A ROUTINE DEVELOPED. We would drive up Friday afternoon after work, come back late Sunday night, hitting the
Lincoln Tunnel around midnight.

Often we went up Route 17 in New Jersey, the prototyp-
ical suburban highway. It is forty miles of Wendy's, McDon-
ald's, Burger Kings, White Castles, White Towers, Red
Lobsters, Olive Gardens, Unos, Applebees, Barnes & Noble
superstores, Tower Records, HMVs, Flemington Furs,
Burlington Coat Factories, Sy Syms, Crazy Eddies, Circuit
Citys, CompUSAs, Lumber 84s, Home Depots, Lowe's,
Sam's Clubs, BJs, Costcos, Gaps, Gap for Kids, Old Navys,
Bed and Baths, Bed, Bath and Beyonds, Tile Citys, Citgos,
and Mobil stations, separated by strip malls and Motel 6s.
Once in a while there will be a regional specialty shop like
Bob's Western Boots. Three acres of manly footwear under
one roof in the heart of cowboy country, north Jersey. A
wedding banquet hall with parking for eight hundred guests.
A shop that just sells white uniforms and orthopedic shoes
to go with them. Route 17 is forever being widened or nar-
rowed or repaired or overpassed or underpassed—each
weekend guaranteed to be a different traffic nightmare. We
learned secret trails around tie-ups in Rutherford, shortcuts
through Saddle River and Paramus. We learned the charm of
driving a human-sized car on the same eight-lane divided
highway next to an 18-wheeler at seventy-five miles an
hour. If we ever get crushed to death, at least we'd know that

it was so that some Safeway store in Piscataway could get their weekly shipment of Huggies three minutes early, and not for something stupid.

Of course, the stores wouldn't be there if nobody shopped in them, and Sue and I made our contribution. Sue would always find some lame excuse to go to the Home Depot. We needed to patch the roof. We needed storm windows. We needed house jacks. We needed grout. We needed Spackle. Half the time I thought she was talking about something she wanted to cook.

"Pick up a little wine, dear, we're having braised grout stuffed with Spackle on a bed of sautéed wild mushrooms."

"Damn, I had it for lunch."

THE FACT THAT there are so many Home Depots should be a warning sign for all home owners. When you tell someone you're renting an apartment they invariably say, "You're just throwing money away. If you bought a house that rent money would all be equity." Wrong. If you buy a house, all that money goes to the Home Depot. Don't believe me? Go try to find a parking space at one. You have to drive around for a half hour waiting for someone to leave. Some of them are open 24/7. In one of them I saw a sign in the lumber department that said, "No wood cut after 10:30 P.M." If enough people were asking that they had to make a sign, you wonder.

The place is full of guys (well, mostly guys) who are going

to install hot tubs and Jacuzzis. Guys who are buying pressure hoses to clean their decks, decks that they built with wood that they bought here and presumably had cut before 10:30 P.M. There are guys buying tools to cut bathroom tile, tools to cut pipe, tools to cut wire.

On one day, waiting for Sue to load up on drywall and plywood, I had to use the restroom, which is about a two-mile walk from the front door, past guys who are buying screen doors, miter boxes, arc welders, PVC pipe, crushed marble, and hardware cloth. I get to the men's room, walk up to the urinal, and it's full of pee. How is it that I'm in a store full of guys who can buy and install a toilet using sophisticated power tools but they can't flush one? What is it about flushing a toilet that men find so much harder to do than installing one?

$\mathcal{E}$VENTUALLY IT WAS time for me to get a new driver's license to replace the one I forgot to renew twenty years ago. It seemed easier to get one in Walleye. Unlike Manhattan, there are no daylong lines at the Walleye office of the DMV. There are no college students offering to stand in line for you for $15 an hour. When I went in, except for the two clerks, the place was empty.

Without studying, I passed the challenging written test with flying colors.

"Is it illegal to drive while sitting in the backseat with the passenger door open?"

"The proper speed through a school zone is—75 mph? 55 mph? 27 mph? 15 mph?"

It was the eye test I worried about. I put my feet on the little footsteps painted on the floor and read the first line.

"E, R, T, W, B."

"Well, that's almost right. Now think, Mr. Mullen, what letter looks like an *R*? A *P!* Yes, that's very good. Now try the next line."

"Z, Q, L, A, N."

"What's round like a Q without the little tail? An *O!* There you go, 20/20 vision."

I was shocked. Where was the scorn? The rudeness? The dismissiveness that DMV clerks are trained for? I wasn't quite sure how to act. Was this a trick? Were they suddenly going to start laughing and say, "Are you serious? You'll never drive in this town"? But they didn't. Ten minutes after walking in I left with a shiny new New York State driver's license.

QUICKLY I DISCOVERED that there were many things about driving upstate that were not covered on the test. Waving, the single most important part of rural driving, was never mentioned.

In Walleye, waving is huge. When you pass a car on the highway, you wave. When you pass the house of someone you know, you wave *and* honk. When you're out of the house, raking the leaves or mowing the lawn, and a car goes by, you wave. No matter that you can't see the driver, that you have no idea who it might be. Wave. You're out shoveling snow, you wave. When in doubt, wave.

Most of the time you're waving at the car, you can't see the person. You know who drives the small red truck and who drives the white Toyota. When Vardon Frasier bought a new pickup truck (bumper sticker: "For a small town there sure are a lot of assholes") no one knew who he was for two weeks. He wondered why no one was waving at him.

Not waving will mark you as the most undesirable type of flatlander. When the 18-wheel bulk truck rumbles by to pick up Al and Abby's milk, wave. When the Agway truck goes by to deliver grain to the Tweedys, wave. When Armstrong goes by in his rusted-out Chevy pickup truck with the golf clubs sticking up the back, wave. When the Caldwells go by, wave. He's ninety. She's eighty-seven. So what they can't see anything. Wave.

I'D FORGOTTEN HOW boring it was to own a car. It was like buying a big, needy, expensive, drooling pet that always needs to be walked, that always needs to go to the vet, that is always humping someone's leg. At least you can pretend the pet loves you. The car despises you.

Between the checkups, maintenance, tune-ups, and state inspections, I was spending more time sitting in Casey's

Garden Tractors & Liquor's greasy, tire-smelling waiting room, reading old copies of *Guns and Ammo* and *White Tail Hunter,* than I was at the farm. I always felt he was taking advantage of my ignorance.

"What do you mean the car needs oil?" I wanted to say. "We just had some oil put in a few months ago. Every three thousand miles? Are you sure? That seems like an awful lot of oil. I wasn't born yesterday, you know." I had to let him know that I wasn't some rube who could be taken advantage of.

Even when it ran perfectly, the car was a pain. I had never pumped gas in my life. The last time I had a driver's license it was done for you. I had missed the whole self-serve revolution. Now every time we pull into a gas station it takes me ten minutes to figure out how to use the pump. Did they pass a law that no two gas stations are allowed to have the same kind of pump? Some you pay inside. Some you pay outside. Some you pay before you pump, some you pay after. Some you lift the handle and turn the lever, some you turn the handle and lift the lever. It's a contest and everyone knows the rules except me. I always park on the wrong side of the pump, pull the wrong lever, get gas all over myself and the car. The car always needs to be washed, it always needs to be vacuumed. Couldn't we just take a cab?

BESIDES WAVING, THE driving exam also neglected to mention anything about the other major aspect of rural driving—high-speed deer avoidance.

Even on the coldest, darkest nights, in the middle of snow-storms and thundershowers, we'd see single lights coming down the highway toward us and wonder who would be out riding a motorcycle in this weather? As soon as they passed us and we could see it was a car with a broken light, the question became, why don't they fix the missing headlight in weather like this?

One Friday night we had just finished our weekly broken light discussion when suddenly Sue stood on the brakes. Only my seat belt kept me from leaving my death mask in the dash. In the middle of road were Bambi, his parents, and much of his extended family. The nearest one was inches away from our left headlight. After a few frozen moments, they snorted and leapt to the other side of the road.

The car would have been a complete wreck if Sue had been a moment slower. I could have ended up with a three-hundred-pound six-pointer thrashing in my lap.

The deer won't stay in the woods because there's nothing to eat and they can't stay in the hay fields because they are too vulnerable, so they spend time in both. That's why they're always crossing the road, for food or water. Scientists call them "edge dwellers." The more trees we cut down—for farms or suburbs or industrial parks—the more edge we create, the more deer we create.

Abby, the farmer's wife, said we were G.D. lucky. She said it's not the one you see that you hit, it's the one behind it. They always seem to move in groups of twos and threes.

There was still one thing I didn't understand. When we were alone I asked Sue, "What does 'G.D.' mean?"

"People don't swear up here. 'G.D.' means God Damned."

"You've got to be F.K."

"Watch your mouth."

OVER THE NEXT few weeks, we dragged the necessities up from the city—silverware, utensils, pots and pans, towels, sheets, carload by carload. Sue would spend her time peeling wallpaper and stripping paint and I would help by pointing out the spots she missed and reading.

Soon it was time to replace my sawhorse table and the barn chairs and get some real farmhouse furniture. It shouldn't be too hard; it's a well-known fact that you can get incredible bargains at these small-town country auctions. We should be able to get everything the well-stocked weekend home needs in two or three weekends. If we accidentally get something we don't like we can always take it back into Manhattan and sell it for ten times what we paid. It should be easy to pick up a few folk art pieces, maybe a Biedermeier chair or two.

THERE IS AN auction every Saturday night at the Grange Hall in Trout Creek. The hall is a square, low-ceilinged space full of old, mismatched church pews. You can bring your own cushion if you like. Stacked floor to ceiling around the perimeter is the stuff that will be sold tonight.

Boxes on top of boxes on top of worn-out dinette sets, and pitted pot-metal floor lamps with fly-specked shades. Out from the back sticks a rusted Hollywood bed frame and one thirty-year-old ski. Trout Creek is not as big or cosmopolitan as Walleye. Half the two hundred seats are taken by townspeople who are here for the free entertainment. Latecomers sit on the foot-thick window ledges in the back, the smokers and teenagers hang outside the front door. Sam Musgrave starts the proceedings promptly at 7 P.M. He has gray hair and a thick body. Recently he has switched from using an old-fashioned ribbon microphone to the over-the-ear type that Madonna and Time-Life operators wear. Sam starts with produce. "Eggs. Who'll give me fifty cents a dozen?" Then house plants and quarts of maple syrup. Finally he gets to the contents of a Catskill County home. A box of old magazines. "Who'll give me fifty cents for the whole box? These are *National Geographics*, folks, from 1977 to 1984, not like that old crap they sell over at Belvedere's. Remember, folks, the more you pay for it, the more you'll like it. Here's a fine-looking Hoover vacuum cleaner. We plugged it in this afternoon and it works dandy. Who'll start it off at twenty-five dollars? Who wants this box of green and brown curtains? Who'll give me five dollah? Three dollah. One dollah. There you go, Bob, one dollar. Do I hear two? Real pretty designs of ivy and fishing rods on them. What's your number, Bob? Forty-nine. Forty-nine for one dollar. I got a police scanner here, we plugged it in this afternoon and it works real good. You know what these things sell for, a hundred and fifty dollars at the Radio Shack. Who'll give me fifty dollars right now? Five? Three? Sold to number—hold up your number, Vardon. Number eighty-four."

We are attending the loaves and fishes of bad taste—we can't believe so much ugliness can come out of one small building. Department store art in out-of-date frames. Salad-Shooters in the original boxes, mixing bowls, fifty feet of used rope, a wheel rim for an '83 Chevy truck, a box of *Reader's Digest* condensed books, a lamp that looks like a clamshell, with a torn shade, a set of plastic hors d'oeuvre picks. This is not wonderful fifties camp. It is not Victorian kitsch. It is not rustic simplicity. There are no Thonet chairs, no Stickley daybeds, no folk art paintings, no moose antler chandeliers. It is discount-store junk that was bought over the last ten or twenty years that was junk when it was new and hasn't improved with age. Oh yes, in a couple of hundred years, someone will collect it and pay good money for it. But in our lifetime it's worth negative money. If no one buys it at this auction they will have to pay someone to haul it to the dump.

SAM MUSGRAVE CONTINUES without a break. "Here's a beauty. A gun rack made out of knotty pine and polyurethaned right up nice. Look at that shine. Do I hear eighty dollah? Fifty dollah? OK, twenty-five dollah. Who'll give me ten? Five? Three? Thank you, Vardon. Look at this, mighty fine pink blankets. They got some holes in them but if you wear socks to bed, what's the difference? I got a— well, what exactly is this, Bob? A leather splitter? I got a leather splitter here in pretty good shape. Who'll give me ten dollah I say ten dollah who's got ten dollah who'll give me eight dollah there in the back I see eight dollah who'll give me nine dollah, nine dollah no nine dollah where? Nine dollah sold! To number 163 for eight dollars. Boys, bring out that box of kitchen utensils. A set of fine old cookie cutters. Who'll start the bid with two dollars?"

AFTER SIX GRANGE HALL auctions the only thing we had bought was a chair with a cane seat that Sue thought she could repair. Counting the ones that had been left in the barn, we now had three and a half chairs. Our car had more seats than our house. My God, we're living in a Loretta Lynn record.

We started going to estate sales, too. This ad in the *Conservative Shopper* sounded promising.

Contents of the Elmington Bradley estate of East Walleye. The house has been in the family for 140 years. All contents in house and barn will be sold. Farm equipment. Hummels. Dolls. Mission furniture. Persian carpets, old photographs, picture frames, mirrors, cherry drop-leaf table, sleigh bed, Avon bottles, Art Deco bedroom suite, tools, fishing gear,

glassware, silver service, collectible toys, teddy bears, can-
nons, several buggies in good condition, model airplanes,
darkroom equipment, household appliances, kitchen equipment. Plenty of bric-a-brac. Three miles off Route 7, follow the signs. Plenty of parking, bring chairs. Cash or good
checks. Harvey Slidel, Auctioneer.

The Bradley estate *has* been in the same family for 140
years. And not one Bradley knew how to use a paintbrush or
a hammer. Instead of following the signs, the ad could have
said to follow the swaybacked, collapsing buildings. Or follow the smell of the thirty cats who have been peeing on the
"Persian" carpets for years. The inside is a museum of discon-
tinued wallpaper and cracked linoleum. Sometimes three or
four patterns in the same room.

The Mission furniture is actually "Mission-type" furniture, and even if the "Persian" carpets didn't smell like the
bottom of a lion's cage, they all had tags that said, "Made in
Canada." Where's the joy in buying something that hasn't
been made by young children in semislavery? The "Art
Deco" bedroom suite is actually 1950s Art Moderne—
splitting, peeling, cheap blond veneer over preformed,
pressed wood with oxidizing brassine handles. "Art Deco"
seems to cover a lot of territory these days—anything between Colonial and Post Modern. But within this rag-and-
bone iceberg there were a few things of interest. A solid
oak lawyer's bookcase with beveled glass panels in beautiful

shape, a piece of Red Wing pottery that the surviving Bradleys overlooked when they looted the place, and a white Hoosier that had been in the kitchen since the day the house was built, with all its original hardware. The Mission-style chair goes for eleven dollars. The carpets they can't give away. A bedroom suite brings in eight dollars. Maybe we should stay. That Hoosier's worth six hundred dollars if it's worth a dime. If we got it for twenty-five dollars, wouldn't we have a story to tell? After two hours we are still waiting for it to hit the block. Harvey Slidel has been selling the contents of the basement—bicycle wheels, Jim Beam bottles, a bench vise, a solitary ski that looks a lot like the mate to the one they sold at the Grange Hall. Finally Harvey's assistants have moved it to the back porch, where he is now selling boxes from the attic. When we saw the Bradleys' everyday curtains and towels we wondered exactly how bad something had to be to make it to the attic. At last, Slidel starts his pitch. "What we have here is a fine-looking Hoosier. Who'll start the bidding at six hundred dollars?" Three hands go up. It's hammered off at seven hundred and fifty dollars to a New York City dealer. The Red Wing pottery goes for a hundred and fifty dollars to a woman who showed up five minutes ago, wearing a short black coat with a monkey fur collar, a white cowboy hat, deerskin mukluks, and large amounts of Elsa Peretti jewelry. After her bid, she picks up the piece and leaves. The bookcase went for eight hundred and twenty-five dollars to a guy who had arrived on a motorcycle, dressed entirely in black leather. I was curious to see how he was going to get the thing home, but Sue had had enough. The rest of the Bradley estate put together didn't add up to a thousand dollars. We went home to our three and a half chairs.

———

*T*HAT SUNDAY WE drove home through an ice storm. It was terrible and beautiful at the same time. The trees were coated with an inch of ice like something from Disney's *Fantasia*. Limbs would crack and fall, taking power and phone lines with them. We followed a sand truck for two hours, passing hundreds of 18-wheelers and SUVs pulled to the side.

NEXT WEEK IS Thanksgiving, and Sue wants to spend the whole week at the farm. I have long held the theory that the Pilgrims were so happy on Thanksgiving because they didn't have to go back to England and spend time with their relatives. Sue and I refuse to go to any relative's house on any of the national holidays. It's gotten too crazy. Instead we spend the day giving thanks we don't have to spend eighteen hours in a crowded airport waiting for the fog to lift in Cincinnati. Giving thanks that I don't have to drive down I-95 at seventy-five miles per hour just to keep up being passed by aggressive drivers. But a whole week in the middle of nowhere? I don't think I can do it. I can't stay away from work that long.

WITH MOVIE SCREENINGS and parties, no one expects to see me in the office every day. I used to fax in my stories, now I e-mail them. Days would go by before I showed up. Now, with the weekend house wasting big chunks of my time, it has been weeks since I've shown up at my desk. I should at least pay a courtesy visit.

"Jim, Jim, come on in!" Melissa motions from her desk. She has the phone on her shoulder and she's typing into the computer. In seconds she's off the phone and we're catching up. While we're sitting in her office talking, a cheery blonde walks in.

"I'm collecting money for Joe's wife," she announces.

"Put me in for ten." The young lady thanks Melissa and leaves.

"What's the matter with Joe's wife?" I ask.

"How should I know? I don't even know who Joe is," says Melissa.

"Then why did you give him ten dollars?"

"I didn't give him ten dollars. I gave his wife ten dollars. I guess you could call it a tip for putting up with Joe."

"But you don't even know Joe!"

"Listen, I've got a lot of work to do. If I don't give something to Joe's wife, I look like a jerk. I have to work with these people every day. That's why I give money. I'll just put in an extra taxi receipt, if it's OK with you. Call it the secret I-work-in-a-big-office-in-a-big-city tax."

There is another knock on the door.

"We're collecting money for Suzy's baby shower."

"Fine, put me in. How much?"

"Twenty."

Melissa pulls a bill from her purse.

"By the way, Bill is leaving to take a job in Florida. Do you want to go in on the going-away cake?" Melissa takes out more cash.

This is pretty neat. Bill not only gets to move to Florida, he gets a new job and a free cake. I am also starting to wonder how anyone gets any work done in an office. I never noticed the interruptions before. Maybe a week in the country wouldn't be so bad.

---

*T*HE WINTER WAS unbelievable. If it was forty degrees in the city it was twenty degrees at the farm. If it was twenty degrees in the city it was zero degrees at the farm. If it snowed an inch in the city, we got a foot. If it rained in New York, we got an ice storm; a breeze in the city took down trees in the Catskills.

Most days it was warmer in that famous cold spot, International Falls, than it was in Walleye. We still had no television; we relied on the world's smallest radio station for the weather.

> *Today's Catskill County ski report from G-100, God's Country radio: Frostbite Valley, twenty trails open, twenty- to forty-inch ice base, half an inch of machine-groomed snow surface, with huge patches of open ground exposed rocks. Widowmaker Mountain, sixteen trails open, twenty-five- to forty-five-inch ice base, one inch of machine-groomed surface covered with rough, scratchy round balls of frozen ice. Deadman's Cliff, ice and loose, stinging, sandlike blowing snow at the base and the peak.*
>
> *Now back to the music. Here are the Rototillers with "Cattle on a Hot Tin Roof."*

EACH FRIDAY NIGHT we'd dash upstate and rush inside to see if we had running water or not. Half the time the pipe that brought the spring water into the house would be frozen. We couldn't flush the toilet and we couldn't take a shower until it thawed out.

"So what, we've got plenty of water," I said the first time. "There's two feet of snow on the ground, all we have to do is melt it." I took our huge pasta pot and scooped it full of snow and put it on top of the woodstove. Problem solved. Jack London, move over. Half an hour later the snow was all melted and voilà! There's a half inch of water in the bottom of the pot. At this rate it should take only three or four days to melt enough snow to flush the toilet.

"Plan B, Jack London calls a plumber."

. . .

THE PLUMBER TOLD us to use bottled water until we can get a well dug because the water line from the spring to the house isn't buried deep enough, and besides it can go dry in the summer. That will be $240, thank you very much.

His advice is to call Walleye Drilling & Pet Grooming (owned by his-brother-law Denton) when the ground gets soft enough to drill a well.

"When would that be?"

"Oh, late May."

---

*W*E MET VARDON FRASIER, a farmer on the far end of Spilt Milk Road, in early March when he stopped by to ask if he could tap our sugar maple trees.

"But we only have three."

"Yes, but they're easy to get to, right on the road. Most of my trees are up on the top of the mountain and when the snow is deep, it's no fun collecting sap. Try walking through two-foot-deep snow trying to carry a sloshing bucket of sap in the freezing cold. It gets all over your clothes, half the time it sloshes into your boots. Course, if it was fun, they wouldn't call it work, would they?"

"But it's March. It's not going to snow anymore, is it?"

Vardon is still laughing.

Vardon, we learned, is the guy weekenders on the road went to for practical things. When hunters get their 4 x 4s stuck in the woods, Vardon is the guy they call on their cell phones for help. He goes up on his big John Deere and pulls them out. He charges them twenty bucks. When my lawn tractor needed to be repaired he told me not to take it to Trout Creek Engine and Carpet Cleaning but to Casey's Garden Tractors & Liquor up on Federal Hill. He knows when it's time to split the rhubarb and the easiest way to plant potatoes. He remembers the old days, when the big money crop in the valley was cauliflower, and tells us that one of Auntie Ellen's first jobs was tying the huge, big leaves of the cauliflower over the plant to make sure it stayed white and wouldn't bolt, and the days, not so long ago, when migrant workers weren't an uncommon sight in upstate New York. He tells stories about his grandfather taking milk to the dairy in milk cans on the back of a horse-driven cart, a horse-drawn sleigh in the winter.

"He was one of the old-timers," he says. "Of course, the farms weren't so big then. They didn't need all this modern equipment. They'd only milk ten or twelve cows a day. By hand."

"The lazy bums," I didn't say.

ONE SATURDAY SOON after, we woke up to see four sap buckets hanging from each of our still-leafless maple trees. I took the lid off one and looked inside. It was half full of clear sap, with a layer of ice on top. I broke the ice with my hand and tasted it. The texture was a surprise. It looked and tasted like water, not thick and sticky as I expected. Vardon showed up later in the afternoon and emptied the buckets into a big plastic container on the back of his rusted-out pickup. We got in our car and followed him down to his sugar house, a dilapidated little outbuilding across the road from his barn with white steam pouring out of a little square cupola on the roof. Inside was a five-foot-by-six-foot shallow stainless steel pan on top of a roaring wood fire. Raw maple sap dripped in one side of the pan, New York State maple syrup dripped out of the other into a five-gallon drum. Vardon let us watch him evaporate maple syrup while I peppered him with stupid questions: how much sap goes in one bucket, how much sap comes out of one tree in one day, how often do you have to collect it, why do the buckets have lids, does tapping hurt the trees, how big does the tree have to be before you can tap them, how do you know when the sap is running, when do you stop tapping, how much wood do you have to burn to make a gallon of syrup, how do you grade it, is there a difference in taste between New York syrup and Vermont syrup and Canadian syrup? I seemed to be asking some of the right questions and he seemed to be enjoying answering them. His wife and his kids would wander into the sugar shack at random, like the cats that mark us and then go eat.

"So you've come up here to live off the grid and avoid the black helicopters?" Vardon asks.

"Black helicopters? What black helicopters? What grid?"

Within minutes we were filled in on the Unified Conspiracy Theory of the Universe, which seamlessly explains the deaths of John F. Kennedy and his son, Lee Harvey Oswald, Robert Kennedy, Martin Luther King, Malcolm X, David Koresh, and Vince Foster by linking them to Area 51, weather balloons, Gary Powers, the Second Amendment, feminists, and fluoride.

I asked why I hadn't read any of this in the *New York Times* and he said it's because they're in on it, of course. Yeah, those newspaper people—they're big on keeping secrets. Obviously, he didn't know any.

HE THREW SOME more wood into the stove that heats the evaporator and told us about what he'll be planting as soon as the ground thaws, the livestock he's planning to buy, and the chicks he had just bought that he was going to raise to eat. I again started asking questions: How long does it take for a chick to get big enough to eat? What do you feed them? How much care is involved? I also wanted to know where he went to buy the baby chicks—is there a store for that, or do you get them from another farmer, or what? So I asked, "Where do the chicks come from?"

His wife, Verbena, arrived just in time to hear the question and exchanged an incredulous look with her husband.

"They come from eggs! I thought even flatlanders knew that!"

I'VE BEEN READING the *Shopper* since we bought the house and usually there are only three or four obituaries each week. This week there were ten. On closer inspection it seems most of these people died months ago. These were notices of committal services.

"The ground is finally thawed enough so that they can dig the hole to bury these people who died in the winter," Sue explained.

"So, the first sign of spring up here isn't a robin, it's a burial?"

One of the death announcements was for Cincinnatus Pliny Tidwell of Spilt Milk Road. I knew everyone on Spilt Milk by now. Who was this?

"Do we know a Cincinnatus Tidwell?"

"Sure, that's Moonbeam."

"The guy who lives in the chicken coop? He's dead?"

Moonbeam was not a hippie, but an old mountain man who'd lived up here since Jesus was a baby. Even the old-timers, the old dairy farmers who had passed the family farms on to their sons long ago, called Moonbeam old. He got the nickname not because he was flaky but because he beamed and smiled all the time, a joyful man. He had lived for many years in an old chicken coop on the highest and coldest spot on our road. The western Catskills are actually a plateau carved into valleys by glaciers, so instead of a peak, the mountains level out on top for hundreds of wavy yards and then fall away into the next valley. The tops of many hills are the best hay fields; they get sun all day, unlike the shadowy valleys.

In early December Moonbeam moved into town with relatives for the winter. They feared he might not survive another winter in the chicken coop on top of the hill with just a woodstove and no running water. So he moved into their comfortable stone house in Walleye, where he had his own room with his own bath. After dinner one snowy February night he took out the garbage and got hit by a pickup truck with only one headlight.

MOONBEAM'S FUNERAL WAS in a huge old white clapboard mansion in Trout Creek. It had three turrets, a widow's walk, a deep curved porch that wrapped around three sides. Make a note, find out why funeral homes are always in the best house in town? It turned out that this was to be the last funeral in the building. The funeral director was retiring and the house was being turned into doctors' offices—poetic justice if ever there was. The place was fascinatingly creepy. Twenty-foot-long red velvet curtains in the parlor; heavily carved Victorian sofas and side chairs; an overstuffed barrel-back chair in the hall; hideous light fixtures made out of pot metal casts of famous works of art—Botticelli's Venus with two tulip lamps floating over her shoulders; elephant-foot umbrella stands; heavy mahogany-veneered Edwardian sideboards.

I ASKED IF the director was taking the furniture with him or letting Sam Musgrave sell it.

"Are you kidding? *I* can sell it for more money than Sam. You want to bid on some of it?"

"Well, that sofa's kind of interesting."

"Gimme twenty-five dollars and it's yours."

"What about that chair?"

"Ten dollars."

"Your kids don't want this stuff?"

"Are you kidding? This is a funeral home. Nobody wants it. It skeeves people out."

"But nobody actually died on the sofa, right?"

"Not while I was here."

"What about this sideboard?"

"I know nobody died on that."

"No, I mean, how much is it?"

"Take it. Fifteen dollars. But you have remove all this stuff by Tuesday."

"The lamp?"

"*That's* gonna cost you. I can't be giving this stuff away. Thirty dollars."

Sunday morning our farm was crammed with furniture. It looked like we'd been living there for a hundred years.

———

$\mathcal{A}$T LAST, SPRING was arriving in New York City. The tulips were out in Central Park, the flowering trees were blooming. If it's this pretty in the city, imagine how lovely it must be in the country. That first April we took the Palisades Parkway up the New Jersey side of the Hudson. The Manhattan skyline through the budding trees, the hills of the

Bronx across the river, the early flowers, daffodils and dandelions. We kept driving, north and west and up. By the time we got to Roscoe, the flowers were no longer blooming. It was March here, not April. In Walleye it was February. Not a leaf on a tree, not a green shoot to be seen. At least it had stopped snowing. It was raining. The ground squished when you walked. A walk to the road to grab the local newspaper, the weekly *Conservative Shopper,* would leave city shoes soggy and useless.

THE *CONSERVATIVE SHOPPER* doesn't print any national news but if you want to know who bounced a check at the Gas 'n' Go or who's late on their property taxes, it's the paper for you. I worried about a lot of things in the big city, but having the *New York Times* print my name if I bounced a check at D'Agostino was not one of them. For two reasons. The New York papers would never cover a crime so petty, and the D'Agostino would never take my check. But because the *Shopper* is so vigilant I can write a check anywhere in Walleye. Without ID. Nothing like the chance your neighbors will see your name in the "Police Blotter" to take a bite out of crime.

For such a tiny town, according to the *Conservative Shopper,* the place is a gangsta's paradise—passing a bad instrument, driving while impaired, fifth-degree possession of stolen property, second degree menacing, fourth-degree criminal mischief, endangering the welfare of a minor, disorderly conduct, possession of a controlled substance. The more serious crimes get front-page coverage. A teenager ran away with his girlfriend. They found his parents, dairy farmers, shot dead in their bedroom, the family car missing. The kids were caught a few weeks later in Texas after *America's Most Wanted* did a story on them. No doubt some clever lawyer will defend them with a "farm rage" defense. A young, off-duty state trooper was shot dead trying to stop a supermarket robbery. A sixteen-year-old girl stabbed her eighteen-year-old boyfriend to death on his front lawn at 8 A.M. one morning and then went to school like nothing had happened. She was found not guilty.

If you go by network television, crime doesn't happen in small-town America. It happens only in the big city. What you do see a lot of on television is stories that start, "What a shame it is that the family farms and the small-town way of life are disappearing."

AS THE DAYS got longer, the lawn and the fields around the farmhouse filled with great, giant, mutant dandelions. The flowers are the size of a bagel and they stand about two feet tall. Why is it so easy to grow weeds and so hard to grow food?

It turns out you *can* eat dandelion greens. If you're starving and there is no sea kelp nearby. Oh, I suppose there's an adventuresome charm in saying you eat them, but just because something is edible doesn't mean it tastes good. In the search to find fresh food in any season, the food scouts have discovered other early bloomers like fiddlehead fern tops, chicory, and kale. I don't think I know anyone I despise enough to serve them to, though.

But isn't there some kind of dandelion wine they make in the country? I found a recipe in the old Euell Gibbons *Stalking the Wild Asparagus,* which I found on the shelf next to *The Last Whole Earth Catalog* and *Five Acres and Independence.* Books I had saved since hippydom when Sue and I first met.

THE WINE RECIPE called for a gallon of dandelion flowers, some sweet fruit, a couple of gallons of boiling water, sugar, and yeast. Move over, Napa Valley.

I filled ten jugs with my own personal vintage and laid it down in the basem—ah, wine cellar. According to the book, it should be ready to drink in October.

I went to get a tool out of the basement a few weeks later. All the bottles either had exploded or had blown their corks and spilled. The smell was a combination of gasoline, compost, and spoiled silage. In several places it had eaten holes in the concrete floor.

IT IS ALMOST May. I'm throwing wood on the fire like it's January in Lapland. Six months ago if you had said to me, "The Catskills," I would have said, "Grossinger's, the Neville, Mount Airy Lodge, Borscht Belt comedians." Now I would say, "Winter." I am typing this in my new furniture-filled office wearing wool gloves with the tips of the fingers cut off and three sweaters on top of a layer of thermal underwear. With the right hat I could play Doolittle the dustman in *My Fair Lady*.

While I'm freezing to death, Sue is running around barefoot in a tank top. When I pile on the covers, she kicks them off. "Is it me," I asked, "or are you out of your F.M.?"

"It's like living a fairy tale," she says.

I WENT TO the A-Mart and bought a dual-control (from that famous electronics company, GF) electric blanket. This way she could turn her side off and I could stay toasty warm. But somehow, the A-Mart had missed the recall notice. On this particular shipment, the controls were switched. They worked, it's just that the left knob controlled the right side and vice versa. The first night we used it, I turned mine up to three. Sue turned hers down to one. I was still cold so I turned it up to six. Sue was dying and turned her switch off. I was freezing so I turned mine up again to ten. Sue kicked it off and went upstairs to sleep. It was while she was gone that I figured out the problem. I will hear about this for the next forty years. But I also realized I had accidentally stumbled on the perfect metaphor for marriage. Turning any knob will always give you the opposite result of what you expect.

• • •

THERE ARE OTHER incompatibilities besides heat sensitivity. I jump out of bed at five in the morning, she straggles out at seven. I have never missed a meal, she forgets to eat. She tells people that I have bulimia but I forget to purge. She can't wait to get in the car and drive to the farmhouse, I can't wait to get in the car and drive back to the city. I laugh when I see that celebrity marriages break up due to "irreconcilable differences." They are such amateurs.

MY HEAT JONES has left us so low on firewood, I've got to get more. But where to buy wood? And how much? One cord? Five cords? Ten cords? What in the G.D.M.F. hell is a cord, anyway? It's like an acre of land—no one knows what it means anymore. It turns out that five cords of wood turns out to be ten pickup-truck loads of logs dumped in a huge pile on the front lawn. As I wrote out the $500 check I asked the guy when he was coming back to stack it. He has a high, clear laugh.

"Oh, that's rich," he said. "The guys at the Big Pig are gonna love this."

I was tempted to say, "I'll make it six hundred dollars if you don't," but I knew he'd take it and tell the story anyway.

It took a while, but I learned how to stack wood. Make a note, wear gloves. If you don't, you might get a splinter the size of an ax handle right in a spot so tender that you might have to go to the O'Malley Hospital emergency room forty minutes away to get fixed. And sit there for two hours next to a weekender who'd driven his ATV through a barbed-wire fence at thirty miles per hour on one side and a farmer who got his shirt caught in his tractor's spinning power take-off on the other. The tractor's motor quit before it could twist him up like the rubber band on a model airplane. But it did take him twenty minutes to cut himself out with a jackknife before he could crawl for help.

I learned to stack the wood carefully, so it doesn't tip over just when Vardon Frasier drives by and you're standing there like a silly fool waving at him. I learned to purchase the wood early enough in the year so that it has a few months to cure, so that when you throw it into the stove it won't explode like a firecracker and spit bright sparks all over the brand-new wool carpet and make burn marks that Sue will notice and not speak to you for quite some time.

I learned that doing mindless, repetitive work gives the mind a chance to wander. The Trappist monks and the Carmelite nuns have been doing it for hundreds of years, forswearing material things in favor of soul-cleansing menial labor. Unfortunately, it seems to have the opposite effect on postal workers.

After a few minutes of stacking log upon log, my mind wanders to those hardy pioneers who first settled the Catskills. They cut the wood by hand, not chain saw; they split it with maul and wedge, not a generator-powered splitter; and they stacked it. And my mind wanders to the fact that if these guys had to go outside to go to the bathroom, you can bet they weren't taking showers *inside* the house. These guys would clean out the barn, shovel shit, toss hay, chop firewood, and then crawl into bed *in* their dirty, filthy, disgusting clothes. Maybe letting your mind wander is not such a good thing.

———

Since the ground had been soft enough to bury Moonbeam, we figured it was soft enough to dig our well. We called Walleye Drilling & Pet Grooming and Denton took a break from pet grooming long enough to walk us around the property looking for the right place to sink it. The septic tank was on the west side of the house so Denton told us the well should be downhill on the east side to avoid problems.

"Actually, we don't drill the well, we pound it out. The water seeps through the layers of rock and fills up the well, but we found by drilling, we would sometimes seal up the cracks we wanted to keep open. This way we don't usually have to go too deep."

At fifty dollars a foot, I would hope not. "How deep do these things usually go?"

"No way to tell. Guy up on top of Federal Hill right now. We're down six hundred feet and we're still only getting three gallons a minute. Need seven gallons a minute, minimum. Twelve is better. Some places I've got twelve gallons a minute at twenty feet. Other places you get sulfur water. Nothing you can do about that. You're at the bottom of the hill, so I'm guessing eighty to a hundred and twenty feet."

"Did I tell you we were on a budget?"

"So let me get my dowsing rods and we'll find the exact spot." Sue and I looked at each other.

"He's kidding, right?"

Denton reached behind the seat of his pickup and pulled out two thin metal rods. They were wire coat hangers that had been straightened out and bent into a long *L* shape. Like a pistol with an extra long barrel. He held the rods straight out, belt high, facing forward, the little bent part held tightly in each fist. He walked slowly across the lawn and every so often the wires would slowly come toward each other and cross. When they did Denny marked the spot in the grass with his heel. A few times the rods crossed and even bent down toward the ground. He again marked the spot with his heel. He crisscrossed the lawn, leaving heel marks in the grass. After a half hour or so, patterns developed in the yard, some in straight lines, some in clusters. He pointed along one path of heel marks. "Do you know if there's a water pipe under here?" We shook our heads, we don't know.

"What about here?" Denton pointed down another line.

"Nothing that I know of."

"Probably an underground stream. I think we should drill over here. I got a really strong pull on the rods right here."

He pointed to a cluster of heel marks about forty feet away from the house.

"You really don't believe you can find water with a couple of bent coat hangers, do you?" I had to ask, he seems like such a regular guy.

"Some say you need the fork of an apple tree that grows on the property, others say you need a water witch, but I say that's a bunch of superstitious hooey. Coat hangers work just as well as wood. Besides, you got to drill somewhere. Its guess is as good as yours or mine."

"Do you mind if I try them?" I asked. Sure enough, with no conscious effort on my part the rods would cross as I walked around the yard.

He struck some water at twelve feet, but not enough. The final well was ninety-three feet deep.

WE TOOK THE three chairs we found in the barn and the half chair Sue bought at auction to the Walleye landfill. In the harsh daylight she realized that even if she restored the finish and recaned the seat it would still look like crap. It would just be too expensive to throw away. We filled the back of the station wagon with the chairs, glass bottles, several different types of recyclable plastic, one bag full of used tin cans, a stack of newspapers, carpet remnants, and peeling linoleum from the kitchen floor.

It's so easy to throw things away in the city. Put an old, knobless VCR out on the avenue and by the time you get

back to your apartment the stuff is long gone. It's like a Road Runner cartoon: the pile gets taken so quickly you'd swear you can still see its shadow. Leave a broken dish drainer on the floor of the garbage chute room and it will disappear in seconds. You won't see who took it, just the sound of a door clicking shut behind you.

In the country it is not so simple. Here, if you want something thrown away, you must take it to the landfill.

Garbage becomes very top of mind when it's your job to get rid of it. I've wasted hours trying to sort and separate. Is a used can of shaving cream recyclable? What about plastic razors? Used plastic deodorant sticks? Those little Styrofoam trays supermarkets put chicken in? And the little half Pamper that it sits on? Free AOL CDs? Printer cartridges? Are they garbage, trash, or crap?

If the Eskimos have three hundred words for different kinds of snow—the thing they have the most of—we're going to end up with three hundred words for trash. We have to put it all in a clear plastic bag so the garbage police can see if we threw any illegal stuff in there. If we have, we could lose our landfill privileges. You know you've hit bottom when you lose your dump privileges.

Stuff that decomposes—fried rice, potato salad, leftover vegetables, my underwear, grass clippings, leaves, coffee grounds—we throw onto our compost heap. Sue keeps telling me that it will turn into good natural fertilizer, but I wonder. If it's that easy to get rid of garbage, why doesn't the city do it? Why are they putting it on barges and sending it halfway around the world?

These are problems we don't have on Christopher Street. There, I can walk out the door in my slippers, scoot down the hall, and toss the trash down the chute. Here, dumping the trash is just one of an endless chain of chores.

Of course, even in the city not everything goes smoothly. I remember visiting my elderly uncle Eddie and his wife, Velma, back in Virginia Beach. They had moved into a modern high-rise after they sold their house. I was taking them to some family reunion and while waiting for Velma to finish putting on her face, Eddie turned to me and said, "This is about my only job now." He picked up a brown paper bag off the table and opened his apartment door. The garbage chute was almost directly across the way. He took the bag and, with an elegant toss, sent it to the incinerator, dusting off his hands as he came back into the living room. Velma walked in and said, "Let's go." Eddie and I headed for the door when Velma asked, "Where did that potato salad I made for the party go? It was in a brown paper bag on the table."

EVERY WEEKEND I was making little discoveries about small-town living. Banking Bob is open on Saturday till noon and all his tellers already know my name. I've been using the Chemical Bank on Sheridan Square for ten years and I've never seen the same teller twice, much less one that knew my name. They lost a $5,000 check on me once and acted like I was the one who made a mistake. I don't have to buy something at a Walleye store just to get change. Shopkeepers are happy to change paper money for me. When people ask for my phone number, I only have to give the last four digits. The entire town uses the same prefix. I don't have to search and search for a parking spot. After parking for seven months in the No Parking zone in front of Smalley's Video and Septic Tank Cleaning while I returned my videos, I finally got a ticket. It was for ten dollars.

I spent a lot of time in Smalley's; they have an entire section of foreign films and *cinema oscuro*.

I was in there looking for *Hagbard and Signe* one Saturday morning when a housewifey-looking woman comes in and returns a stack of tapes. She's thirty-fiveish, short hair, perky—the average-looking small-town mom. Smalley asks her if she liked any of the videos.

"Well, I liked *I Cut Out the Lying Bastard's Heart with a Dull Knife* but *Make It Look Like an Accident* was unwatchable. No one would believe that was an accident. There were a few good parts in *Crawl, Beg, and Die,* but *Stab Him Silly* had no production values. Did *May Dismember Wedding* come in? No? How about *Woodchipper Momma? Meat Grinder Madness?* I'll just take these, then, *May Worms Eat His Innards* and *Bad Women, Good Lawyers.*"

I kept a close eye on the "Police Blotter" in the *Conservative Shopper* for the next few weeks, but there were no suspicious, widow-making accidents reported.

———

$\mathcal{A}$L AND ABBY, our dairy-farming neighbors, invited us to dinner. Big food, farm food. Fried chicken, biscuits, mashed potatoes, gravy, homemade pickles, homemade pies and whipped cream. There are big glistening glasses of whole milk on the table, plenty of butter. Alvin grew the corn and milked the cows, Abby killed the chicken, made the pickles, and cooked the pies. Just the sight of it would give all the anorexics at Balthazar the dry heaves. Absolutely delicious.

It is strange how things change. A hundred years ago you could make a society woman faint by mentioning sex; now all you have to do is serve her high-fat food. You can talk about sex with women all you want without a tad of embarrassment. Hell, you can have sex with them without embarrassment. As long as you're careful not to mention you still eat bacon.

Al is fifty-six and the operation to replace his knees last year didn't take. He hobbles from his house to the barn on crutches. He looks like one of those black-and-white Walker Evans WPA photos of dust bowl farmers. Long, deep character lines in his face, a one-day stubble, and some days an empty look in his eyes. Other days he'll be into leg pulling and joking as if he's getting away with something in the back of life's classroom while the other kids are studying. Al has only two fingers on his right hand. He lost the others thirty years ago trying to clean out the corn blower. Abby says he didn't even go to the hospital. He wrapped his hand in a handkerchief and told her about it when he got finished with chores that night. What do you need all them fingers for, anyway?

He and a hired man do the thousand and two odd chores that keep a farm running: measuring out grain and corn for each cow according to the nutritionist's instructions, mending fences, spreading manure, fixing the hay wagons, repairing the baler, emptying the silos, picking stone, planting, fixing machinery, plowing, unjamming the silo unloader, helping cows freshen, fixing the barn cleaner, chopping the corn, baling the hay, milking the cows twice a day.

There are seventy cows in the milk barn and at any moment one or more of them are noisily excreting copious amounts of shit and piss. It hits the concrete floor with an audible splat spraying excreta in all directions—under the cow, on the cow's udders, on the back of the cow's hind legs, on the legs and haunches of the neighboring cow, on any flatlanders standing around, on Al. The stench is acrid and sharp. Unlike the earthy charm of horse manure, cow manure stinks. In an enclosed place like a barn, it is a chemical weapon. If you spend over twenty seconds in there, the odor clings to you like sand to a bathing suit. The farmers refer to it as "the barn." If a dairy farmer drops by and you invite him into your house while they are still wearing work clothes they will usually say, "Thanks, but I've got the barn all over me." What they should really wear in the barn is a space suit with its own oxygen supply.

BEHIND EACH COW hangs a long piece of baling twine with a small noose at the end.

"What are those for?" I asked the first time I was in Al's milk barn. Al grabs the manure-covered cow's tail that has just smacked me in the face and puts the end though the loop.

"To keep them from hitting *me* in the face when I milk."

"What happens to the cows when they get too old to milk?"

"We call the meat wagon," he explains. "Sometimes we call the meat wagon if the cow's a troublemaker, or if she's had two stillborn calves in a row. It's hard enough to raise normal cows, who needs a troublemaker? So they take the cow to the butcher and we get the meat or we sell it. But it's not like you make any money on the deal. I sent a calf in the other day and after we paid the shipping I got a check for fifty-three cents."

SUNK INTO A gutter in the floor of the milk barn there is a chain-driven contraption called a barn cleaner that runs in a large circle around the barn, moving the manure down the trench with little blades, and dumps it into a wagon called a manure spreader. Twice a day, Al drives it up the steep hills onto one of his many fields, where he spreads it. The wagon is equipped with a little gate and a spinning propeller that shoots the thick, gooey manure into the grass, fertilizing the field and getting rid of a lot of cow manure at the same time. It also spreads the smell quite effectively on nice hot summer days. The two times a day Al does this are about the time Sue and I have breakfast and dinner.

LIKE ALL OUR farmer neighbors, half of Al's land is straight up and down. None of it is level. It's very beautiful but it beats down the equipment. And it's dangerous. In the wet spring and early summer, tractors are always slipping and sliding. Once a year one will turn over and crush some hardworking farmer to death. They say it is more dangerous to be a farmer in this country than to be a policeman.

For all his work, Al gets about thirteen cents a gallon for milk, the same price he got in 1972.

I asked him if he'd heard about the farmer who won ten million dollars in the state lottery. They asked him what he was going to do with all the money and he said, "Well, I guess I'll just keep farming until it runs out."

Al didn't laugh.

Sometimes Abby won't see anyone but Al for days. So when you finally do talk to her, her conversation can come out in great bursts. As we ate, I asked her how her trip to town went today.

"It's full of summer people. You wouldn't believe the traffic. The light turned twice before I could get to the post office. And then I had to go around the block three times for a parking space. I wish all these flatlanders would just go home instead of coming up here and making our lives miserable. I ran into Arnie from the road department and he said there's talk of putting in a *second* light! Did you ever! And who's going to pay for that, I'd like to know? Just another rat hole to pour our money down, if you ask me. And the line at the grocery store. It's worth your life to try and get a cart. And the prices. And you can't get out for love nor money. They got that Morley girl working the cash register. She was the one that fell off the back of the pickup truck on prom night and she ain't been right since. Not that I have much use for any of them. Her sister was the one that married that Newcomb character. It's no surprise to me that he's in jail. I had a cousin that went to school with his younger brother and he was at their house once and said the place looked like thunder. After dinner, he said, the kids would just turn over their plates to keep the flies off them till morning. Nothing ever got washed . . ."

Just then the lights flicker and die. In the sudden quiet we can hear a large piece of machinery somewhere off in the distance wind down, like a big saw blade spinning slower and slower till it stops. HMHMHM-hmmhmm-hmmm—hm—h——m——m. The regular hum of the fridge is gone; the light buzz of the water pumps, gone. Abby finds an oil-filled hurricane lamp, lights it, and puts it on the table. We continue dinner as if nothing had happened.

The power goes out so regularly, at least once a week, that it's barely worth mentioning. Anything can cause it. A thundershower, a wet snow, a windstorm, a Tuesday. The worst is when it flickers on and off for half a second. Just enough to make you have to reset every electronic clock in the house—the answering machine, the VCR, the microwave. It takes me days to get them all back to normal. Why they put clocks on some of these appliances is a puzzlement. Do we really need a clock on a toaster? On a Dustbuster?

Sometimes it goes out for hours. Sometimes more. The longest outage I can remember was twenty-four hours, but usually it doesn't stay out long, forty-five minutes, an hour.

The first few times, if the phone worked, we'd call the power co-op and wait around nervously for someone to show up. What about the food in the fridge? What about the food in the freezer? Just about the time we dug out some ratty old candles from the jumble drawer and tried to get them to stand up in the middle of a saucer by dripping wax on it, the lights would come back on. No one from Rural Electric ever showed up. We had to get something better than smelly, dangerous, and ineffective candles. No wonder Milton went blind. Try reading a book with a candle. You almost have to put the flame between yourself and the pages to see anything. Plus they're dangerous. It's hard to believe there is a building in the country from the colonial period still standing, with this kind of fire threat in it every night for hundreds of years.

Soon we figured out that if we were without power, everyone on the road was without power. Let *them* call the power company. The house is now scattered with old-fashioned hurricane lamps that we light when necessary. It's a break in the routine, and kind of romantic. We learned that you get much more light if you put the lamp in front of a mirror, something that was probably common knowledge before Edison. What is not so romantic is that you can flush the toilet only once when the power's out—the water pump is electric.

Dinner was over, Abby was serving pie. There was black-berry, early peach, and pecan. The lights came back on.

Al pushes himself away from the table and grabs his crutches. "Time for me to get back to work."

"Need some help?" I volunteer.

"Yeah," he says, "I got a cow about to freshen. You want to help deliver it?"

"Yeah, let's ah, oh, I forgot. My doctor told me never to put my hand in a two-thousand-pound cow after a big meal."

NINE O'CLOCK SUNDAY night, we pack the car, lock the house, and leave. I still don't like the three-hour commute each weekend. Which is odd because I sleep most of the way while Sue drives. I suffer from a little-studied condition called car lag.

There is very little of interest on the drive down. The only thing that changes from week to week is the graffiti written on the freeway overpasses and the high rocky cliffs. "Go Cougars" or "$\Sigma\Delta\Omega$" or "Gary & Sally." One favorite spot for the kids is on a big piece of bedrock sticking out of a field facing the thruway near Harriman. This week the graffiti were gone, covered up by a coat of gray paint.

Can you imagine what would have happened to anyone who painted over these if they had been Native American petroglyphs or aboriginal paintings? What makes today's messages any different? How do we know that the Anasazi little dancing man wasn't the indigenous people's version of "Go Cougars"?

We pass housing development after housing development as we get closer to the city. One week it's a pasture, the next week it's Bottled Water Estates. "Attached town houses from $120,000." Shouldn't a town house be in town, not fifteen miles from the nearest crossroads?

It is everything you can do not to say, "I remember when this used to be a cornfield." That may be the most common phrase in America. You will hear it anytime there are two or more people in the car. And it makes the people in the car profoundly sad. Not because the cornfield is now another sprawling mall or a housing development or a hideous gas station—minimart. Not because it represents the disappearance of the family farm or the loss of a connection with an earlier, simpler time. Not because acres of cool, nurturing, green earth have been turned into hot, steaming, soul-killing concrete. The people in the car are sad because they didn't have the brains to buy this cornfield twenty years ago.

"If we had bought that land, we'd be rich right now. We'd be rolling in it. We'd be sitting on the beach right now drinking Bahama Mamas working on our tans. If we were smart, we'd buy everything that's still a cornfield. You just know that twenty years from now today's cornfields are going to be new malls, new car dealers, new industrial parks."

Many people say it's a damn shame that we're destroying our open spaces and wildlife habitat for future generations, but then, what do you think your future generations would want? Wide open, unspoiled countryside, or bags of money left to them by Grandad and Grandma, who invested in housing development projects and tax-deferred REITs? You bet they want the money. And I think we all know what a boon to society inherited money is. People who inherit lots of money lead richer, fuller, deeper, more meaningful lives than the rest of us. Well, maybe not the Du Ponts, the Kennedys, and the Rockefellers. Or the Dukes, the Vanderbilts, or the Windsors. But I'm sure you can find someone out there who inherited a lot of money and is happy about it—it's just that none come to mind right away.

"Yep, if we had bought that cornfield twenty years ago, our kids could have the things we never had. They could have grown up with all the advantages. Nice clothes, fancy cars, skiing vacations. They could have grown up to be like all those snotty kids we hated when we were in high school.

And they would have thanked us for it. Like those Menendez brothers thanked their parents. Yes, I can remember when this was a cornfield. A useless, unproductive cornfield."

Will there ever come a day when we'll drive past a corn-field and say, "Remember when this used to be an ugly, un-necessary minimart?"

THERE IS A note from the co-op board shoved under our door advising us that it is expressly forbidden in the co-op bylaws to have sex on the folding tables in the laundry room.

"Do you think they sent this to everyone, or just us?" I asked Sue.

"I don't care. All I know is that we're doing the laundry at the farm from now on."

Sue has to spend this week at the convention center attending something called the Yarn Fair. I decide to put in some face time at the office. The E train is packed. The head-line on today's *Post,* which everyone is reading, says, "Mayor Dinkins to Lay Off 6,000 Workers!" The ad over our heads on the train says:

We're Hiring!
New York Public Schools Want Bilingual College Grads
Qualified as
School Psychologists
Social Workers
Teachers of Special Education

Teachers of Speech Improvement
Guidance Counselors

New York City public school students are reading two years below grade level. Am I the only one to notice they want everything but regular classroom teachers?

I CLIMB OUT of the subway at Fiftieth and Broadway and head for the office. Safety at last, the employees' entrance. But my ID card won't open the door. Am I another casualty in the mysterious Midtown Triangle—a place where people you don't know ask you for money, a place where men on the street try to sell you Rolex watches for $6, a place where all electronics stores are "Going Out of Business"— or could it be something simpler, like if I don't use the card for a few months it's automatically canceled? It's anybody's guess. I go around to the main entrance. There is a new receptionist at the front desk. I can't get her to believe I work here.

"I've been here for six months, and I've never seen you." Her hand is under the desktop, buzzing furiously for security. "Besides, everybody knows Jim Mullen is a fake name they use for stuff the staff writes." A burly guy in a blue uniform is coming toward me. So, this is the dark and ugly side of telecommuting that no one wants to talk about.

"Jim!" It is Melissa, who grabs me as she saunters by. "It's just been crazy here. They're having this blood drive today.

I've never given blood before, so it was all new to me. I go down there and this nurse, she's Asian and has kind of an accent and she tells me to roll up my sleeve and make a face. So I roll up my sleeve and go all bug eyed and wide mouthed and she says, 'Make a face, make a face.' So, I close one eye and stick out my tongue. She still says, 'Make a face.' Now she's getting angry. 'Make a face.' Finally, it hits me that she's saying 'Make a fist.' I was so embarrassed."

Nothing had changed. It was like not seeing one of those afternoon soap operas for six months. You could tune in and know exactly what was happening even though you had missed 120 episodes. Ralph still had the shrine to Princess Di on his desk. A foot-tall color statue of Diana in a deep blue, floor-length gown in a plaster of Paris grotto, embedded with flamboyant seashells. In front of it are several Princess Di ashtrays, "limited edition" plates, coffee mugs, and key chains. He threatened to sue the company once to get the day off on Diana's birthday because it was a religious holiday for him. What does he ask for when he prays to her? "Dear Diana, can you please send me some twenty-thousand-dollar ball gowns immediately? A pearl choker would be nice too. Your biggest fan, Ralph."

Larry's office walls are still full of framed, meaningless inspirational messages.

"Say it with confidence and most people will believe you."

"When in doubt, fire someone."

"Synergy—it sounds better than Conflict of Interest."

A temp is sitting in my cubicle. "I'll move," she says.

"No, I'm not staying. What have they got you doing?"

"The boss's expense account. I like it except for all the overtime. I think they're going to need two of us."

Some things never change.

THE QUITTING SMOKING was still not going well. I wouldn't smoke during weekends in the country, but back in town, the temptations were too strong. One or two drinks with Rob Corona and before the night was over I'd be back on the Philip Morris plantation. So I was trying to avoid him for a while. It didn't stop him from calling me on the phone.

"I had to go to the post office yesterday to pick up this month's *Vogue*. It was too big to fit in my mailbox. I don't understand it. Everybody in Manhattan has the same size mailbox, so of course everybody in the city has to go to the post office and wait in line to pick up their issue. How convenient. Has it ever occurred to them to split that thing up and send it out twice a month? It's the size of the phone book. Pissed me off."

"Isn't Bob Geldof planning a charity drive for you guys, people who are too busy to pick up their mail?"

I told him I couldn't meet him for drinks. Now that I wasn't here every day, I made an effort to enjoy the city. I walked straight down Sixth Avenue from midtown.

I stopped when I got to Bike City at Eighteenth Street in Chelsea. Now, there's something that would keep my mind

off cigarettes, I thought. I knew what Sue meant about keeping her hands busy. I, too, wanted something to fill up all the
time on my nonsmoking hands, but working like a field hand
isn't my idea of fun. There was a bike in the window they
called a hybrid, half racing bike, half mountain bike. It had
thin racing tires but regular *T*-shaped handlebars, not like
those ten-speed torture machines that drop down and make
you assume an obscene Yoga position while you spin. If God
had wanted us to have our butts several feet higher than our
heads, he would have put them there. These new bikes were
different. This one had a multicolored paint job, quick release tires, the latest in space-age, self-propelled technology.
You could lift it with one finger. Twenty-one speeds with the
shifters at your fingertips, light as a feather, and with a
choice of saddles.

The salesman tells me that he rides twenty miles every
day before work and one hundred miles on the weekends.
He has 2 percent body fat. You could play handball on his ass.
And for big fat me to have a body like that all I have to do
was ride a bike? You mean have fun and lose weight?

"Make sure you buy a good lock if you plan to ride it in
Manhattan," the clerk advises as he writes up the sale. I've
lived in Greenwich Village for twenty years, thank you very
much. I know a thing or two about personal security. I
picked out a chain with links as thick as my thumb and a
two-pound padlock. So much for buying a lightweight bike.
If the bike didn't work out I could take up competitive

yachting; I already have the anchor chain. As I'm buying this, a Rasta man bike messenger walks in: yellow skin-tight Spandex top, black bike shorts, huge dreads. He points to the chain and says, "You buying *that* little t'ing, mon? Well, I guess it'll keep your *good* friends from stealing it."

The messenger and the shop owner give me tag team advice on bicycle thieves. Don't chain the bike to a parking meter. Thieves have pipe cutters; they cut the head off the meter then lift your bike right over the top. Try to lock it to a tall tree or a signpost. After you lock it, take the seat with you. Then if someone cuts the chain and tries to ride it away, it won't be comfy. Don't take your eyes off it. If you're riding it to work, take it up to the office with you.

For the first time, for a quick moment, I actually felt depressed about being a New Yorker. I've been spending my weekends in a place where I could leave a bike on the front lawn for a week and it would still be there when I got back. My dreams of riding down to the Strand bookstore on a sunny afternoon, spending hours browsing, then hopping back on my trusty bike for the quick, invigorating ride back to the apartment were quickly fading.

"First t'ing, mon, buy some black electrical tape and wrap it round the whole bike, man, like mine. Make the t'ing look all old an' beat. Nobody want it then."

"Oh, that's the other thing you've got to watch out for," says the shop owner. "Bike jackers. You'll be riding down the street and suddenly the car beside you will open the passenger side door and stomp on the brakes. You can't stop, so you hit the door and fall off the bike. They scoop it up, throw it in the car, and drive off while you're lying on the ground with a broken wrist or worse."

"You're kidding. That doesn't really happen."

"It hoppen to me twice, mon."

I rode the bike home from the shop, my first time on a bike in maybe thirty years, and I'm riding in Manhattan traffic? Six blocks from home I realize another mistake I have made. The charming cobblestoned streets of the West Village are pretty to look at but they are a teeth-pounding, butt-breaking ride. It's like being in some kind of bizarre consumer product test where they shake things to see how long they last. I threw the bike in the trunk of the car and took it up to the farm. I never rode in the city again.

SUE SHAKES ME out of bed. We had driven up to the farmhouse through a dense, eerie fog. It had taken two hours longer than usual.

"There's a six-foot-by-three-foot-by-six-foot-deep hole in the raised beds. I went up to plant all that stuff I started in the house and there's a big grave up there."

"And you're saying it wasn't there last weekend?"

"I'd have remembered something like that."

"Do you think someone was trying to put something in, or do you think something crawled out?"

Soon we are both out in the backyard staring into a perfect, rectangular hole. The edges look as if they have been cut with a knife. The sky is gray, there is a dense and miserable mist. Is that the howl of an evil presence I hear in the distance? No, that sounds more like a whining engine and it is getting closer. Out of the cloud rides the Hulk on a four-wheeler, though none of the four wheels seems to be touching the ground at any given time. He jumps off and walks up the hill to our garden faster than I can run. He sticks out a huge hand. Mine disappears into his for ten or fifteen seconds.

"Oh, 'tis a grand pleasure to finally be makin' your acquaintance," says he. "You being Mr. Mullen, I take it? And the missus." He doffed a nonexistent hat.

We've fallen through the Celtic time-space continuum into *The Quiet Man*. It's Squire Danaher come to life. This is the farmer on the other side of us. We see his herd grazing from our kitchen window. He's been here forty-five years now and his brogue has settled down to Barry Fitzgerald times two. I apologize for not coming over and introducing myself sooner but "we're only up here on the weekends."

"So am I, man! I live in Hartsdale. This is what I do to relax!" I wanted to ask why he needed to relax if he lived in Hartsdale, but then I pictured that huge hand around my throat and was granted the wisdom to be quiet. But surely his was a working farm. I have seen his cattle, his horses, his hay, his tractors, his cars and trucks. I have seen everything but the squire.

"It's beef cattle, man! They take care of themselves!" At the time, I knew no better and turned my palms up and mouthed "Oh," as if that explained everything.

Almost every sentence he spoke had an exclamation point at the end. He's twenty years older than I am and has five times the energy. He stared into our newly discovered grave.

"I see you've found the problem," he said.

"What is the problem?" Sue asked.

I began to suggest some possibilities out loud. "It could be a lot of things—ritual satanic child sacrifices, zombie jamborees, college hazing ceremonies gone terribly wrong, the undead rising to make their rightful claim among the living, a pack of wild dogs with glowing yellow eyes searching for unclean things they buried long ago . . ."

"It's my spring," interrupted the squire before I could really get rolling. "It cuts across your property here. The pipe broke this week past. I had time to repair it, but not fill the hole. I'll bring my backhoe down this afternoon and fill it in."

"You have your own backhoe?"

"And it causes more problems than it's worth. Last week I was down digging a new drainage ditch for my low field and I climbed down into it to fix something, I don't even remember what, when I slipped and got my foot caught under a great huge stone. I'm down there yelling for help but the backhoe is running and no one can hear me over that and no one can see me in the hole. It took me four hours to work my foot out from under that G.D. rock!"

• • •

MY FIRST REAL ride on the new bike was down Spilt Milk Road to Al and Abby's house, maybe a half mile, round trip. It took forty-five minutes of starting and stopping to catch my breath. The rest of the weekend I lay in bed and coughed up gray-green slime. It was something they could have used in *The Madness of King George.* When did that hill in front of Abby's house become so steep? It's unnoticeable in the car. I've read that when Americans go to a shopping mall, they won't park more than six hundred feet from where they want to go. If it's farther than that, they'll get back in the car and drive to a closer entrance. Now I know why. You'd think it would take more than forty years of doing next to nothing to get this out of shape. The next weekend, I rode to Abby's house again. It took only thirty minutes and I coughed up slime for only a couple of hours. The next weekend I got up the hill *past* her house. No coughing, very little slime. Gradually I could stay on the bike fifteen minutes before gasping for breath. After about a month and a half I could go a half hour straight. I hadn't had a cigarette in a month. I was so proud of myself. Only eighteen months after I quit smoking, I quit smoking.

SOON, CATALOGS SELLING bicycle equipment started arriving in the P.O. box, filled with pictures of healthy, skinny eighteen-year-olds in skin-tight riding pants and Giro touring helmets. They looked so happy, so healthy. Soon I

had the turquoise gloves, a Day-Glo yellow helmet, a fire engine red nylon wind shell. It took me forty-five minutes, but
one day I rolled up to Vardon Frasier's farm, huffing and
puffing and feeling quite proud. The odometer on the handlebars reads five and a half miles. His dogs start barking and
he walks out of his barn to see who's here. He looks at my
getup and yells over his shoulder, "Honey, get the kids! The
fat Power Ranger is here!"

I COOKED HAMBURGERS in the backyard tonight, the first
time I'd done that in twenty-five years. They came out all
mangled and torn, half burnt and half raw. Do you flip them
a lot, or do you flip them a little? Is the grill supposed to be
very hot, or just hot? Do you leave the grill cover up, or do
you put it down? Do you squish them down, or leave them
alone? I couldn't remember. Fortunately, it didn't matter,
they tasted exactly the way they were supposed to. It must
be impossible to screw up ground beef—that's why they let
men run the grill. I know there are books on how to grill,
and backyard chefs always think they know the best way to
cook. But it is all a sham made to make men look more in-
telligent than they are. Why had it been so long since we had
grilled a hamburger? They taste great, they're easy to cook.
Why weren't we doing this every day?

Because that's why we moved to Manhattan in the first
place—to get away from hamburger America. To get away
from lawn mowers and cul-de-sacs and *McCall's* and *Redbooks*

and *Reader's Digest* condensed book collections. We didn't want to deal with cars and crabgrass and waste our precious time on a thousand other little trivial suburban things when we could be wasting our time on a thousand little city things—traffic jams and crane collapses and stalled subway trains. Mowing the lawn, grilling hamburgers, waving to the neighbors? How hopelessly hokey. Maybe we can do it again tomorrow.

———

Sue AND I are no longer speaking. It's Friday. We left our apartment at five thirty. It is now seven forty-five and we are on Twelfth Avenue at Forty-sixth, maybe two miles from where we started. On the radio they have said, "Give us twenty-two minutes and we'll give you the world," eight times already.

If I *were* speaking, I would say, "What's the rush? Each week for the past three years we've been doing this when we could have stayed home, watched the news and *Entertainment Tonight,* ordered General Tsao's chicken, relaxed a little bit like civilized people."

If she *were* speaking she would say, "Because it wasn't like this last week. It only takes one stalled car to jam up the whole works. Why are you blaming me? It's not my fault."

And I would say, "Who's blaming you? I'm saying why do we have to rush out the door like crazy people every Friday afternoon? The country's still going to be there if we get there at nine o'clock or ten o'clock, so what's the rush to go sit in traffic for three hours?" But we both know if we have this discussion it will be the last time we speak without lawyers present. We both have the good sense to sit there and seethe.

The traffic is so slow, there are men walking in between the cars on Twelfth Avenue selling roses, hot dogs, newspapers, and novelty toys. There is also some plain old-fashioned panhandling. There are police everywhere. They are actively ignoring everyone. They have more important things to do than arrest panhandlers and direct traffic. Not that they're actually doing anything more important right now, but they might have to at some vague date in the future. We watch the hansom cab drivers return their horses to their stables. We watch the huge Caribbean cruise ships moored at the West Side piers. We are trapped; we can go neither left nor right, forward nor back. Something has got to change.

WE AGREED TO start coming up on Thursday nights. It gave us an extra day at the farm and we would miss the weekend traffic. Many times we'd take a Monday off, too. I could do my job anywhere with a fax machine and a computer. Sue cut back on her hours.

With the extra time at the farmhouse, Sue started planting an even bigger garden. Six or eight different types of tomatoes. Yukon gold potatoes, blue potatoes, broccoli, cauliflower, radicchio, arugula, four types of corn. She dug an asparagus trench. Strawberries, rhubarb, currant bushes, raspberry vines. Basil, lemon balm, borage, dill weed, catnip, and mint. We are talking a big garden. Maybe a quarter of a football field. It's totally organic. She's planted marigolds around the tomatoes to keep the aphids out and she uses some natural concoction to keep away the squash bugs. But the thing that makes it work is manual labor. Instead of spraying weeds, she pulls them; instead of insecticide, she'll pull the bugs off plants. She's out there till dark, every night, till nine thirty or so in the summer. I couldn't believe the amount of rocks I had to watch her move before she could plant anything. The locals say the ground has "two rocks for every dirt" and that's understating it by half. I told her we should paint a sign on the barn, "Rocks for Sale. You Pick 'Em, Half Price." She said I should go mow the lawn.

"Do you think this is fun for me?" I asked. "Watching you work? I thought you bought this place to relax."

IN THE CATSKILLS microclimate you can't plant anything until after the last frost in June. That could come on June 1 or June 15, but come it will. The first frost in fall can come in early September. Which means that if you're lucky, you have ninety days to grow things in the ground. It's such a short season, most plants must be started indoors. The farmers buy special fast-maturing corn. They try to stretch the season by planting it in mid-May and hope all the frosts come before the tender sprouts start poking out of the ground.

April through May, every flat surface in the house is covered with Sue's bedding trays. Every windowsill, every tabletop has something growing on it. There is not enough room on the dining room table to open the *Conservative Shopper*.

"I'm not the kind of person to complain, but isn't there some other place you can put these?"

"*You're* not the kind of person to complain? All you do is complain. It's too hot, it's too cold, we never go anywhere, we're gone too much. You bitch about having to watch TV for a living. You work one day a week and then complain that you don't get enough vacation days. People with real jobs want to have you killed."

"You're changing the subject. These plants have got to go. It's cruel to keep them in captivity like this. They are begging for their freedom. They long to be in the wild. *Born free*," I sing, "*as free as the wind blows, as free as the grass grows. Born free.*"

"Your work here is finished. It's time to go destroy someone else's life."

"You laugh, but I know Al and Abby aren't growing baby plants in their kitchen right now."

"First of all, I'm not laughing. Secondly, Al grows feed corn and hay—the two things that you can almost grow out-

doors up here. Everything else needs help. To do this prop-
erly, I should really have a greenhouse."

"Then get a greenhouse. How much could they cost, anyway?" They could cost $9,000, that's exactly how much they
could cost. Make a note, never open your big, fat, stupid
mouth again. It's not the money, but it seems that everything
we buy is for chores, not for fun. Wagons, pruning shears,
hoes, shovels, spades, splitting mauls, battery chargers,
muck boots, hacksaws, jumper cables, miter boxes, fan belts,
work shoes, work pants, work coats, work gloves, work hats.

Who wants to do that much work? How come we aren't
buying tennis rackets and golf clubs? Now I know why J. D.
Salinger hasn't published anything in forty years. He bought
a house in the country. He probably spends all his creative
juices mowing the lawn. Have we escaped the phony hell of
the Hamptons just to join the non-phony hell of Catskill
County? While making fun of the idle rich is my reason for
living, I can't see that being busy and poor is preferable.

For all the money we were spending on the house, with
the exception of the little greenhouse, none of it was visible.
We added no west wing, we had no cathedral-ceilinged
great room. It was still a modest little farmhouse, nothing
fancy about it, even though we were slowly plowing every
cent we had into it. For what it took to modernize the bathroom, and for the new foundation for the mudroom, the
new well, for replacing the roof on the barn, replacing
boards and battens on the back of the barn, for new win-

dows, new clapboards, chimney repair, for rewiring from top to bottom, for a new furnace, we could have built a new house.

Every day there is something new to fix. In the city, when something breaks, we call the super. Leaky faucet, call the super. Elevator breaks, call the super. Door lock doesn't work, call the super. Tap water's brown and sticky, call the super. How many times had I come home from errands loaded down with heavy bags and trailing some dry cleaning, to find the elevator out of service? To find the door buzzer not working, the intercom on the fritz? We don't know how it's going to be fixed or when, but it will get fixed.

At the farm, we know *exactly* when something's going to be fixed. As soon as we fix it. Here, *we* are the super. The roof leaks, we fix it or find someone who will. When the spring that supplies the water runs dry, we get a well dug. When mice get into the mudroom because there is no foundation, we build a foundation. It's almost as if we're in charge of our own lives.

In the city, even great wealth is no guarantee of control. Paying $8,000 a month rent does not mean the elevator will run or that there will be hot water. Simple errands become Greek epics. Having the platinum American Express card in your pocket will not let you cut in line at the movie theater; the dry cleaner will still destroy your clothes; you cannot make the line move any faster at the D'Agostino.

There are a thousand and one things beyond your control. How much time should you budget to get to the airport? One hour, or three? You have no say in the matter. How well you drive, how much money you have is irrelevant. If a truck jackknifes on the L.I.E., your Wall Street bonus won't get you past it. It is a force above and beyond. Ask not for whom the backup at the toll plaza applies, it applies to you.

NOT THAT EVERYTHING in the country is under our control, either, but the things that aren't tend to be little things. Literally little things. Bugs. Every fall, black flies invade the house and then commit suicide trying to get out. Attracted by the light, they bang into closed windows over and over and over again till they finally knock themselves out. At night, they come to our reading lamps, bouncing off the lamp shades in an annoying tattoo, making it impossible to read in peace.

July is earwig season. Open the medicine cabinet in the morning and five or six of the little pincer-tailed insects will fall into the sink. Pick up the sponge off the sink and two will scurry away. After the earwigs come the ladybugs trying to get indoors for the winter. There are ladybugs everywhere—crawling on the ceilings, climbing up the walls, flying into your hair. It's like walking into some bad made-for-TV horror movie—*Wes Craven's Hideous Homemaker*. "The house looked normal on the outside, but inside it was filthy and disgusting!" Sometimes the only way to get away from all the bugs is to go outdoors.

"Count your blessings," said Vardon Frasier. "At least we don't have cockroaches up here." I don't know if that's a good sign or not. I thought cockroaches could live anywhere.

———

*I*T IS MID-AUGUST. The crops are finally coming in. Sue's tomatoes should be ready to eat next week, the corn maybe a week later. The potato leaves are big and green; she's already picked a few cucumbers. All day long we can hear Al out cutting and baling hay. Sometimes we hear him come down the hill an hour after dark, working by the lights of his tractor.

SUE GOT OUT some hamburger for the grill today in some strange wrapping I didn't recognize.

"Where'd that come from?"

"Abby gave it to us."

"Gave it to us? What an odd pres—no! Do you think it's . . . ?"

"Yeah, heifer burger."

"I don't think so! Was that the little red-and-white one? I knew that cow! I feed pigweed to that cow! It does smell like hamburger, though. It is less fatty. Hey, that's not bad!"

I feel like a cannibal.

. . .

VARDON FRASIER'S HOUSE sits on the site of the original house that burned down after little Damian knocked over a space heater while trying to handcuff the dog to the sofa. "It was the worst thing that ever happened to me in my life," he said. "All my deer heads were lost. Every one. But luckily no one was hurt. Well, it might have been better if little Damian had gotten singed. Not enough to hurt him, but just to teach him a lesson."

The new house started out as a mobile home, but over the years it has had so many porches and bedrooms and mudrooms and decks added to it that it has become an architectural goiter. Outsider art on a grand scale. The Kennedy compound as built by Howard Finster. Nailed to the fading, gray, unpainted plywood outer wall is a chain mail of overlapping hubcaps and license plates that Vardon has collected over the years. There is a paddock made of bits and pieces of farmsom and junksom—a fence gate made from a car hood, the remains of a snowmobile spouting flowers from its missing seat, several giant tractor tires buried half in the ground as a jungle gym for the kids. There are three mangy dogs that Vardon has trained to chase cars as they come down the road, slowing traffic down to a crawl. "Sure, we lose a few dogs, but better them than the kids."

The door is always open, someone is always home. There are three TVs in the living room, one for the picture, one for the sound, and one for video games. A police scanner is squawking. In Catskill County police scanners are like toasters; everyone has one.

Thirteen-year-old Luscious is getting her 4-H project together on the middle of the floor, "Manure: Where Would We Be Without It?" Little Damian, twelve, is where he's been for the last eight weeks, on the recliner. He gets the body cast removed next week and may be allowed to return to school if the investigation into the jungle gym accident clears him. In his lap is a black cat that only he can pet, named Whitey.

AUNTIE ELLEN LIVES there, too She grew up on this farm, as did her mother and her mother's mother. She is three or four thousand years old and a walking *Old Farmer's Almanac*. Oh, and did I mention she is completely out of her mind?

"Firewood burns best if you cut it during the first quarter of the moon," she told me one day.

"You noticed that, too," I said.

"It's a fact."

"Some guy sold me wood cut in the second quarter. I must be some kind of meshuga." She ignored my impertinence.

"If snails come out in February they will stay home in March," she countered.

"Wait, that makes the whole Groundhog Day way of predicting the weather obsolete."

"Beware the pogonip."

"Who doesn't?"

"St. Patrick's Day, plant the peas."

"I wanted to but I was drunk."

"The snow in March will be as deep as the icicles."

"Won't that hurt my peas?"

"If it thunders on April Fools' Day, we'll have good crops of corn and hay."

"Anything about radicchio in there? Does that hold for kohlrabi, too?"

"When chickens have been eating out in the rain, that means two more days of rain."

"You don't watch Al Roker, I take it."

"The first three days of April were foggy. That means a flood in June."

"Who needs that silly old radar?"

"A snowstorm in May is worth a wagonload of hay."

"I think I saw that on Broadway. 'A big, bouncy musical,' says Clive Barnes."

"Never put a broom on a bed or someone will die."

"Is that a hard-and-fast rule, or more of a guideline?"

"If your corn shucks harder than usual, prepare for a cold winter."

"As much as I can with that crappy, second-quarter wood."

"Expect a frost six weeks after the katydids chirp."

"Never use a bungee cord that's a foot too long."

"For headaches, rub cow manure and molasses on your temples."

"That makes my nose hurt and my stomach queasy."

"For digestive ills, eat a spider."

"Sorry, my HMO doesn't cover arachnids."

"No need to burn the barn to kill the flies."

"Are you the one that does the home schooling around here?"

Auntie Ellen had gone out of her mind shortly after her husband died. Once a week she calls the volunteer fire department saying that the Petersons are trying to kill her by pumping gas into her house and then shooting flaming arrows at the roof. They are trying to murder her because she knows too much. She does know a lot, but it's hard to believe the Petersons would kill her to find out her secret for digestive ills. She still calls, but the fire department no longer shows up.

VARDON IS IN the kitchen, canning.

"Taste these, taste these, I think I got something here." Vardon forks out a string bean from a quart canning jar. Behind him Luscious shakes her head in warning. They taste great. Crisp, fresh, yet strangely tangy. Hot even.

Sue has become a big canner, too. All kinds of pickles, her own salsa, jams, and my favorite, apple pie in a can. She makes a ton of apple pie filling from apples in the backyard and cans it up in quart jars. All winter long, all she has to do is make a crust, pour in the filling, and voilà! I'm getting fatter.

. . .

"I MADE THIS batch with pepper flakes. What do you think?" Vardon asks.

"I think you got something." My mouth was starting to feel hot. Very hot. Uncomfortably hot.

"They grow on you, don't they? I got the recipe off the Internet."

"Fiver, niner, niner, one. Reservoir Road," squawked the scanner.

"What does that mean?"

"Ambulance call. Probably a heart attack, with all the old people living on that road."

The scanner continues to blurt out its messages. Sure enough, it's Mr. Block suffering from chest pains. They'll take him to O'Malley Hospital for observation and treatment.

Next to the scanner is Vardon's computer. It sticks out like an American car in the Hamptons. It is the one thing in Vardon's house that was not bought at the Grange Hall auction. The kids' bikes, the sofa, the dining room table and chairs, the freezer, the fridge, the beds, the curtains, the carpet, even the canning jars were all bought from Sam Musgrave auctions over the years.

When Auntie Ellen went crazy, Vardon took over the cooking. He turned out to be a good and enthusiastic cook. Before she got sick he couldn't have made a hot dog. Within a month he was making soufflés and ragouts.

"All them eggs, I might as well raise my own chickens," he said. He planted cucumbers and made his own pickles. He started a serious garden. One month he realized that he loved garlic. In went twenty rows of garlic. Hard neck. Soft neck. Baby garlic. He found some of Auntie Ellen's tomato seeds that had she saved from 1952. The seeds were of an heirloom strain that does particularly well in our short, cool summers. He got a bumper crop. Now he spends almost no money on store-bought food.

"Auntie Ellen says it's going to be a long, cold winter this year."

"How can she tell?" I asked. "The thickness of the squirrel fur? The width of the caterpillars' stripes? The color of the fall leaves? The way the beavers fixed their dam?"

He gave me a look that said, "Flatlander!" and said, "She knows because everyone has a lot of wood stacked up in front of their houses. What do caterpillars' stripes have to do with anything? Is that how you guys predict weather down in the city?"

The peppered beans he has fed me have gone critical.

"What kind of pepper did you put in there?"

"Oh, I don't remember. They were a funny color, though. Yellow, not green or red."

I couldn't speak. Habanero peppers. I'm trying to remember, are they a hundred times hotter than jalapeños, or a thousand times hotter?

Just then I hear Sue's voice. On the scanner. She's on the phone with Beverly.

"You can hear our phone conversations on that thing?"

"Not all of them. Just when you're on the cordless phone."

"Were you ever going to mention this to me?"

"I nearly did the other day. You've got to watch your mouth, boy. There are children in this house."

I PEDAL HOME from Vardon's to warn Sue about the phone. When I walk in, she gives me a cherry tomato she picked from the new greenhouse. She has grown it herself and it is the first tomato of the season.

"Well, what do you think?"

It tastes remarkably like a cherry tomato, the kind you could buy in any big grocery store for, oh, $2 a pound. Yet I sense it would be huge mistake to say that. A life-changing mistake. She has worked, she has sweated for this. I cannot stop myself. I've got to get counseling.

"It is amazing, it tastes like no other tomato I have ever eaten, probably better than any tomato anyone in the history of the world has ever eaten. How did I of all people get the honor of eating such a wondrous fruit?"

Sue's arms are crossed, she is tapping her foot. She gives me that look my teachers used to give me just before they kicked me out of class. But I figure this tomato cost me $9,000. It ought to taste good.

MELISSA WAS SUPPOSED to call me from the office after lunch today, but I didn't hear from her until almost four.

"What is the problem down there? If I miss one more deadline, they'll take away my company car."

"You have a company car?"

"Can't you tell when I'm joking?" I asked.

"Nobody can."

"That is cold. So where have you been?"

"When I came back from lunch, they weren't letting anyone back into the building. There was a suspicious package in the lobby.

"So the bomb squad sends in this remote-controlled robot to pick up the package and put it in the bombmobile out in the middle of the street. It's the size of an ambulance. The streets are blocked off for a six-block radius, traffic is messed up for hours. I had a perfect view of the whole thing. Very slowly the robot comes out of the building holding a package in one of its claws. It's a box wrapped in brown paper about the size of a briefcase, maybe twice as thick. The robot goes across the sidewalk and down the curb, and after it goes about two feet, it stops. Very slowly it lifts the package up over its body and then it starts smashing it onto the street. Up and down, smack, smack, smack, as hard as it can. The thing just goes berserk. Cops are flying over cars, trying to get away; people are running down the street screaming. Finally the box breaks open and it's toner for a copy machine. Some delivery boy has left a box of toner in the lobby. And all I could think about was—not that it could have killed me, not that I could have been maimed—all I thought was that if it had been a bomb, if it had gone off, if a bomb that size had gone off, it couldn't have caused half as many problems as trying to remove it did."

Once again I wonder how anyone gets any work done in the city. It's not that there is one interruption after another; the city itself *is* the interruption.

ON THE TEDIOUS Friday-night drive, twenty-two-minutes-and-we'll-give-you-the-world announced that the price for milk was at an all-time high: $14 a hundredweight. It meant Al might be getting fifteen cents a gallon instead of twelve and a half. The announcers actually called it "white gold."

I couldn't wait to tell Abby that she was married to one of those "wealthy" dairy farmers. The next day I found her in the driveway washing her nine-year-old Buick. The mats were spread out around it and she was standing there with a garden hose, spraying them down.

"I just hope I'll be able to use it again." she said. "Remember that day I gave you the hamburger? One package must have gotten away and rolled under the seat. A few days ago something started to smell funny but I just thought it was a skunk or something. Now the car's been out in the sun for two days and I can't get in it for the stink. I found a two-pound package of ground beef under the front seat."

I decided to wait until she was in a better mood to tell her the good news about milk prices.

I HAD MY own problems. I was very disappointed with our apple crop last year. If you found the Macs from the trees in our old, untended orchard for sale at the supermarket, you would never shop at that store again. They were small, misshapen, dirty-colored things with spots and stains all over them. None of them were apple shaped. Sometimes when I was mowing the lawn I'd grab one, find a clean spot, and take a bite. It was good, but not good enough to stop eating store-bought apples. I used to pick the fallen ones off the ground and dump them over the fence for Al's heifers, but he asked me to stop. He said the apples ferment in one of the cow's four stomachs and it makes them woozy. I don't know if he was pulling my leg or not, but I stopped.

Somehow I got the bright idea that the problem with my apples was that I wasn't spraying poison all over them. That would stop all the bug bites, the tiny blemishes. I bought a gallon can of pesticide with a sprayer attached. Little Miss Organic was against it, but she's not a big apple eater. Besides, how bad can it be? The commercial growers use it all the time. They must use more of it than I will, and I rarely see two-headed children in the produce department of D'Agostino. Is it such a sin to want nice pretty apples? Sue made that little I-give-up sign with her hands and walked away. She honestly thinks I'm too stupid to do this. Please. I think I can manage. But she had me thinking. For once, I read the label on the can.

Before spraying LiquidDeath™ on fruit trees, please take these simple precautions. Make sure all children and pets stay indoors with the windows closed for the next three weeks (21 days). Preferably they should be sent away to relatives in another town way downwind. LiquidDeath™ should not be used by or near pregnant women, or by women who intend to become pregnant in the next 22 years. LiquidDeath™ should not be used near livestock, vegetables, or foodstuffs. If accidentally ingested, call a funeral home immediately. Make the best deal you can. *Note:* Funeral home employees should wear latex gloves while handling your body.

To apply: Wear a self-contained breathing apparatus, like a space suit. Spray apples. Run away as fast as you can. Take off space suit and dispose of it as you would any other class 5 HazMat. Be sure not to touch the suit while you are taking it off. Should you touch the suit, jump into the shower and scrub down like they did Meryl Streep in *Silkwood*.

Should strange lumps appear on your body, especially in the groin area, within two weeks, call our help line, 1-800-DEAD-MAN-WALKING. By using this product you waive all your rights to sue us for any reason, including loss of body hair, rectal bleeding, facial tics, and loss of feeling in feet and/or hands.

It occurred to me that I could probably get a better crop by pruning and fertilizing. Maybe I should plant some new trees. These things were ancient. Besides, I like those newer varieties—Fujis, Crispins, Honey Golds. I'll buy a few of them and see what happens.

————

S UE FIGURES THE FEWER people who know our street address, the better. So we get our mail in town at a post office box.

The mailbox is always jammed with catalogs. Hold Everything, Williams-Sonoma, the Chef's Catalogue, Brooks Brothers, L. L. Bean, Lands' End, Crutchfield, Performance, MacWarehouse, Campmor, Barnes & Noble, Sherry-Lehmann, Musician's Friend, the Metropolitan Museum of Art gift store, the PBS video catalog, Burpee's Seeds, Johnny's Seeds, Balducci's Fine Food, Country Curtains, the MOMA gift store, Northern Tools. There are three or four copies of each one. One to J. Mullen, one to Jim Mullen, one to James Mullen, one to Susan Mullen, one to S. Mullen, one to Sue Mullen, and one to S. Molehead for good measure. There's no point in trying to stop them. If you call and complain they'll send you another copy in yet another variation of your name. While I'm throwing away the eighteenth catalog addressed to S. Molehead I hear someone at the customer service window complaining. "Sheesh," he says to no one as he stomps out. "It's a good thing they don't run businesses the way they run the government." Yes, I'm thinking, let's let these catalog people run the government. There's no telling how much social security S. Molehead would rake in.

At the risk of getting even more junk mail, we still order from them for exotic seeds and equipment we can't get locally. I ordered a new disk drive for my computer by catalog. I called the 800 number and gave the guy our P.O. box number, but he needed the street address for UPS. I said it's kind of complicated, I live on a farm.

He was shocked. "They have farms in New York?" he asked.

WE SEE OUR little deer friends almost every day eating in Al and Abby's hay field. We know they've been in the yard too because we see their droppings under the apple trees. Between the turkeys, the grouse, groundhogs, rabbits, chipmunks, skunks, raccoons, possums, coyotes, and the deer we could be living in a *Wild Kingdom* episode. Every now and then we'll see something more exotic, a wolf or a fox or a mink. Three hours from New York City. Who knew?

It's so peaceful, we try to discourage visitors without being rude about it. Sue will be on the phone and suddenly yell, "Jim, kill that thing!" Then she'll turn her attention back to the caller as if nothing had happened. Sometimes she'll say, "Hang on a second—Jim, when is Lyme disease season again?" She will mention the garden snake the cat caught. Except in her version it's a copperhead. She'll work in the story about the skunks in the compost heap and the rabies scare that's going around. If that doesn't work she gives directions to the farmhouse that make Dollywood sound cosmopolitan.

"You go two and a half miles past the burning tire dump, make a left onto the dirt road unless it's raining. You have four-wheel drive, don't you? With a good, high clearance? OK, you'll see a sign on the left that says, 'Deer Cut-Up.' Go about a mile past that and turn right at the house painted green and pink. When you see the falling-down barn next to an old dilapidated cemetery, make a right. Go past the burned-out double-wide and drive under the high power lines for about ten minutes. None of you have pace-makers, right? They say the cancer cluster on our road is just a statistical fluke and it has nothing to do with the elec-tricity in the wires. I'm sure Jim would have caught the bladder cancer no matter where we lived. That his hair fell out in three weeks, they chalk up to stress. Still, I get a mammogram once a month. You should, too, after the visit. Still, it's not like you have young children with you, or I'd flag you off. When you see a yard full of fifty or sixty wrecked snowmobiles you know you're getting close. If there are only twenty-five or thirty snowmobiles you're on the wrong road." She's kept all but the most determined from visiting. But after Beverly and Bert Ferguson's visit she simply says, "No way."

• • •

WE HAVE HAD bad guests before—the Hadleys come to mind. Ira was a photographer friend who called to say he and his wife would be in the area. Oh, I said foolishly, you must come and spend the night. They arrived and we met his wife for the first time, and the four of us sat around the dining room table for a catch-up chat. After about fifteen minutes Leeza Hadley stood up and asked directions for the bathroom. As she left the room she turned to Ira and said, "Watch my purse."

Before dinner, Sue asked Leeza to help out and mash the potatoes. Leeza looked into the pot full of boiled tubers and said, "I didn't know you could make mashed potatoes out of potatoes. I thought they came out of a box."

COUSIN MOIRA AND her kids came to see the leaves one weekend in early October. One of the kids picked up a fallen apple from the trees in our backyard and started eating it. Moira was appalled. She slapped the apple from the kid's hand and admonished him, "Don't eat that, you don't know where it's been." It may have been the only time in the child's life when he did know where his food had been.

The Bensons weren't any prizes either. They arrived at ten o'clock on Friday night and they wanted to go out to a bar. Sue and I didn't know what to say. We were getting ready for bed. We've been here for three years and we've never gone to a bar. Even if there were one closer than seven miles away, it would never occur to us to go there at ten o'clock at night. Coming to Catskill County to go barhopping is like going to SoHo to go crop dusting. The Bensons think the country is like Central Park. After you spend a little time there walking the dog, you go back to your normal life.

THE FERGUSONS, HOWEVER, raised insensitive guesting to the Olympic level. Bert, Beverly, their two problem children, and Tiny, the St. Bernard. I don't mind having my face licked, but it bothers me that he has his paws on my shoulders when he does it. "Isn't he friendly? Everybody just loves him," Beverly told me as the dog romped through Sue's almost-ready-to-be-picked cherry tomato vines, the vines she had fussed over and nurtured all summer long. Then Tiny came back to the center of the lawn and left a huge gift.

The Fergusons' van was packed with luggage. They were here for a weekend and they were pulling enough things out of the van to stay for a year. Pillows, a dog bed, an electric guitar, portable CD players (one for each member of the family), CDs, suitcases, duffel bags, Doritos, Snausages, and what appeared to be the femur of a mastodon. "Tiny's chew toy," explained Bert. The only thing they seemed to have left behind was their largest pieces of furniture and a few carpets.

"If they're trying to get away from it all," Sue asked, "why did they bring it all with them?"

"We got lost coming up here," says Bert. "My God, this *is*

in the middle of nowhere. I thought you were pulling my leg, but we stopped in a gas station in a town with a very silly name. Bosco or something. We asked the attendant where Walleye was and he said, 'You know where Woodchuck Lodge is?' and I said you must be kidding. Of course not. Then he says, 'You know where Fish's Eddy is then?' I couldn't stop laughing. Then he says, 'What about Bovina?' I thought he was making this stuff up. As if I would be caught dead knowing where a place called Bovina is. Really. Of course, he didn't think it was funny. He says, 'Have you heard of Albany? Rochester?' I told him that I *had* heard of Albany. I said, 'I couldn't tell you where it is, but I am sure I've heard of it.' Then he said, 'Flatlanders!' and walked away. It's no wonder more people from the city don't come to visit you. The people up here are just plain rude."

AT DINNER THAT evening we learned that like all kids of her age and station, Cartier is a vegetarian. Not a problem; if there's one thing we have on the farm it's plenty of vegetables. Right out of the backyard. Or out of the greenhouse. We are the Six Flags over Veggie Paradise. We eat so much zucchini, I'm turning green. Of course, we never eat any of the good-looking vegetables. Those go to neighbors and friends. Sue and I eat the stuff with nicks and dings and woodchuck bites taken out of them. Sue says they taste the same, but they don't. Yes, Cartier has come to the right place to be a vegetarian. There is only one problem. Cartier doesn't like vegetables. She eats peanut butter and jelly sandwiches on white bread. McDonald's french fries. Potato chips. Pop-Tarts.

"Why don't you just stick your face in a can of Spam?" I said. "It'd certainly be healthier."

SUE COOKS IN the country, something she rarely does in the city. Saturday morning, Sue made the Fergusons a "simple" country breakfast. Blueberry buttermilk pancakes with berries she had picked with her own hands, with Vardon Frasier's maple syrup, cantaloupe and watermelon from the garden, toasted homemade bread with strawberry-rhubarb jam that she had made this spring, apple cider made from the fruit of the trees in the backyard. We were ready to eat at eight. The Fergusons got up at eleven.

FOURTEEN-YEAR-OLD Bresson was the first to comment on this bounty. "Don't you have any Pop-Tarts?" Nine-year-old Cartier chimed in with, "Mom, can I have some Count Chocula?"

"This margarine tastes funny."

"It's butter, sweetheart."

"I don't like it."

"This syrup tastes bad. Don't you have any Mrs. Butterworth's?"

We finish up breakfast around noon. Beverly helps Sue clear the table and starts shoveling half-eaten pancakes into the sink. From the dining room I can hear Beverly's half of the conversation. "Is your garbage disposal broken? You're kidding! How do you live without one? A compost heap! Wait till I tell everyone. This really is camping, isn't it? I admire the way you can live like this, I really do. No help, only one bathroom, no latte machine. Cartier! Bresson! Pay attention now! This is how the pioneers lived."

"SO," I ASKED the kids, "what would you like to do today?"

"Watch TV."

"That's wonderful. I would have guessed you were going to say robbing 7-Elevens, but it seems you've been raised by stricter parents than usual. Spare the rod, spoil the child."

"What's a rod?"

"You must let me show you sometime."

"So, what *are* we doing today?" asks Cartier.

"*We* are stacking wood, watering and weeding the garden, washing the dishes, mowing the lawn, cleaning the bathroom, doing the laundry, fixing the cellar door, painting the barn, moving rocks, digging a drainage ditch. Want to help?" I ask.

"Oh no," says Sue, "leave that for the cleaning-stacking-watering-painting fairy. You guys go to the county fair, the kids will love it."

Oh yeah. I can see these two blending right in. Bresson has a ring through his eyebrow with a chain in it that connects to his left ear. A tattoo on his skinny biceps says, "Eat

Shit and Die." His hair is dyed black and shaved bald on one side. He is wearing an oversized T-shirt that comes down to his knees and a pair of black denim shorts that come to mid-calf. Each leg is the size of a hoop skirt. The T-shirt advertises a band named E-Coli in large letters of what appeared to be raw ground beef.

Cartier, like most preteens, is wearing clothes that look like they have been donated from the Chamber of Commerce. There is a logo or a cartoon character on everything.

JUST THEN AL comes down the road pulling the manure spreader.

"Look, honey, it's a farmer on his tractor," says Beverly. The Fergusons watch him pass the house, turn into his field, and start shooting his organic fertilizer over the hay field.

"What's he doing?" Bev asks. Sue and I don't quite know what to say. Within seconds that distinctive odor fills the house. Sue is merciless. She starts talking about what she'll be making for lunch.

"Who likes cabbage?"

"What *is* that?" asks Bresson.

"It's a green vegetable, like lettuce."

"NO! That smell!

"That's the smell of money, son." I could not stop myself. It took me forty years to realize my dad had been joking all that time.

"'Brown gold' we call it. Farmers are rolling in it. You and I, we have to work for a living, but Al, he just waits for his cows to give manure. That's living."

THE FERGUSONS GO upstairs to change for the fair. Beverly comes downstairs wearing black Spandex leggings, a huge printed blouse, and a baby blue turban. Sue takes one look and asks, "How will Jim find you if you get separated?"

Bert is wearing what he thinks are country clothes—ostrich skin cowboy boots with silver tips on them, brand-new blue jeans, a skin-tight cowboy shirt with silver collar tips, a string tie, and a large white hat. He looks like Miss Kitty's pimp.

IN THE FAIR parking lot, a kid with a safety orange flashlight wand motions us to a parking space. The day is hot and dry; cars from as far away as Sidney are on the road. I spot neighbors left and right coming and going, and wave to them as we make our way to the entrance. The first stop is always the 4-H hall. Kids from all over the county bring in their projects—canned pickles, jams, jellies, corn that they've grown, chickens they've raised, ag projects they've worked on like "How to Raise Aqua Poultry." The judging takes place on the first day of the fair, so by the time we get there, a week later, the vegetables are looking pretty sorry. The carrot greens have wilted, you can't tell the bok choy from the corn. Cartier and Bresson have no trouble disguising their boredom. They are making gagging noises. I pretend they are not with me. We move to the midway. Mom, Dad, and I amuse ourselves trying to flip a ball into a floating frog's mouth, which the children find hopelessly hokey.

AT THE BARNS the kids start to show a little interest. Here are the prize-winning animals from farms around the county. Huge guernsey, holstein, Belgian blue, belted Galway, and Black Angus cows, pigs, goats, and at the far end spectacular giant rabbits. The animal judging and auction takes place all during the fair, so the kids who raise them live with them—feeding and milking them, keeping the stalls clean and the bedding fresh. It has kind of a tailgate party atmosphere and the 4-H-ers are about the same age as Cartier and Bresson. While they don't understand anything about animal care, they understand every thing about teenness. The farm kids loved the way Bresson looked. They told him they wished their parents would let them dress that way. Near the dairy barn is a milk house where the kids take their show cows for milking. As we walked by we saw Luscious Frasier strapping the milking equipment on a cow. She oozed a healthy, smart, sexy, funny charm. She was wearing big baggy overalls over a white T-shirt. Her sleeves were rolled up and one overall strap was hanging at her side. Someday she wanted to ride horses and be a vet. Bresson couldn't move.

"Can you really milk that thing?"

"Can Patsy Cline sing?"

"Who's Patsy Cline?"

"You're not from around here, are you?" she asked. They both laughed.

"You gonna help, or you gonna stand there?" she asked Bresson.

"I don't know how," he said.

I introduced Bresson and told him to catch up with us over at the Meadow Muffin Madness. He gave me a puzzled look.

"I'll explain it to him," Luscious said. As we walked away Mom and Dad both asked me what I was talking about.

"Only the biggest event of the fair," I told them. "They take a fenced-in meadow, maybe half an acre, and mark it off into squares about a yard on each side. Then they let three cows into the pasture. Each cow has a number, one, two, and three. You buy a chance that one of the cows will make a plop in your square." Cartier thought this was the funniest thing she had ever heard.

"Dad, he's pulling my leg, isn't he?"

"Of course he is, darling, there's no such thing."

"If cow number one hits your square you get a thousand dollars. If cow number two hits your square you get five hundred dollars, and if cow number three comes in, you get two hundred and fifty dollars."

AS WE'VE BEEN walking we've been passing booth after booth selling ice cream, funnel cakes, blooming onions, Italian ices, curly fries, corn dogs, sausages and onions. The smell is making everyone hungry.

"Is there anywhere we can get some good hummus?" Beverly wants to know. "Or maybe a pasta salad." I steer them to the Big Pig booth. There is a line a hundred people long to get to their order window. Outside the Big Pig's kitchen trailer are ten picnic tables packed with people eating gigantic platefuls of barbecue pork.

"Are you sure they have hummus?" Beverly questions.

"Most definitely. The best hummus you ever tasted." Slowly the line passes the picnic tables. I wondered if Chef Bob had ever even heard of hummus. Up close we can see and smell the food. The pork chops are two and a half inches thick. With a side of BBQ pork and a glob of yellow mashed potatoes. Finally we are close enough to read the menu— the double-pounder with cheese, BBQ pork with a side of pork chops. Surf and turf, a thirty-six-ounce ribeye steak with a dash of sea salt.

"That's funny," I say, "they must be out of hummus."

"Who wants hummus?" asks Beverly. "Do you think one plate of chops is enough, or should I get two?"

"WHY DON'T YOU get a horse?" Cartier asks on the way home. "I'd like to ride a horse."

This from people who can barely take care of a dog. Have you ever seen those gigantic bags of dog food at the grocery store that weigh five hundred pounds? You wonder how anyone can get them home and you wonder about the animal that eats it. Think what it is to take care of an animal like that, to walk an animal like that, to groom an animal like that, to scoop up the shit of an animal like that, to plan your vacations around an animal like that.

If I've learned anything on the farm it's that dumb animals need constant attention. On the other side of Trout Creek there is a man with buffaloes. They are something to see, thirty or forty of them in a Catskill mountain pasture. The fence that keeps them in is something to see, too. It is right out of *Jurassic Park*. The fence posts are the size of telephone poles, with five strands of high-tension electric wire strung between them. During one of the regular random power outages, the herd went right through the fence. It took four days to round them all up.

"YOU HAVE GOT to get them out of my hair," Sue whispers.

"*I've* got to? They're your friends, too."

"Friends? I don't know these people."

"They'll hear you."

"We're in the barn."

"Cartier was in the bathroom for two hours, flushing the toilet over and over and over again. Whatever it is she's doing in there is simply beyond me, but how a septic tank works is not a discussion I want to have with a ten-year-old. You have got to get them out of here before everything we own is rubble. This morning I caught that dog with a big gray chew toy. About an hour later I noticed the elephant foot umbrella stand was missing. The thing's a menace. Twenty years in the city and I never used that pepper spray in my purse. I hate to think that the first time I use it will be on my own houseguests."

"Maybe we should rethink turning the barn into a guest house."

"Can it be finished by tonight?"

"I meant in the near future. By the way, why did you hang towels over the bathroom window?"

"I didn't, the Fergusons did. They're afraid someone will see them in the shower."

"Kids."

"No, Bert and Beverly."

"Who do they think is going to see them? Nobody could see them with binoculars."

"They're your guests. You talk to them."

"My dad always says, 'If you need curtains, you're still in the city.'"

"Good, get your dad up here to tell the Fergusons they're in the country."

"They're leaving tonight. I'll keep them out of your hair until it's time to go."

Sue prepared a vegetarian dinner that night featuring dandelion greens, fiddlehead fern tops, chicory, and kale. The Fergusons were packed and loaded before dessert. They wanted to stay, but they really had to get back.

. . .

AFTER THAT, WE stopped telling people how much we liked living up here. When old friends ask about the farm, we complain about the snow, the radio reception, and the bad dirt roads. We tell them about the $9,000 tomato, the dandelion wine exploding all over the basement. We tell them about the septic tank.

WE HAD VOLUNTEERED our house to have a surprise birthday party for Abby. No one arrives fashionably late for a party in Walleye. You say seven and that's when they show up. Six fifty-nine is considered early and 7:01 is just plain thoughtless. And don't worry about cocktails and hors d'oeuvres. The guests expect dinner to be on the table. Instead of people asking Sue for the recipe she'll hear things like, "I never had lasagna before," and, "I've always heard you could eat asparagus but I never knew anyone who actually did." A green salad will go as untouched as the centerpiece. Dinner should be beef or ham. Chicken they can eat at home. If you want to be really experimental you can go with roast pork, but people will talk. Vegetables should be creamed, potatoes should be mashed. Anything that cannot be improved by Campbell's cream of mushroom soup should be avoided. All desserts must contain either Jell-O, Cool Whip, or miniature marshmallows; the best ones have all three.

In the Walleye supermarket there is a tiny section of one

shelf called the "fancy food" section. It has such exotica as whole peppercorns and dried oregano.

ABBY AND THIRTY of her friends have crammed themselves into our house. It was a great success, Abby was mightily surprised. As were we when the toilet stopped working. I found out when Sue pulled me aside and asked why Vardon was out peeing in the backyard. A good question.

Vardon told me my septic tank probably needed pumping. Nothing would go down.

Word had gotten out quickly. To everyone but us.

"I am so embarrassed," I said. "Of all the nights to happen."

"That's all right, we expected it. Everybody came prepared. You don't see none of the women drinking anything, do you? We all knew it had to happen sooner or later. This house is pretty old. You were gonna have to get a new septic system sooner or later."

"Vardon, I don't even know what a septic system is."

"I suppose you don't. It's like this. Out here in the country you're not hooked up to a sewer system like you are in the city. Everything goes into a big holding tank—a septic tank—buried in the ground. And the bacteria live in the water and break down the solids. On the far side of the tank is another pipe, which takes the broken-down wastewater out into a leach field, a bunch of pipes that spreads the water around and lets it gradually soak into the ground. As that water leaches down through the soil, more bacteria keep breaking it down into nutrients. Finally, the only thing left is clear, clean water."

"Then why isn't mine working?"

"Oh, lots of things. In the old days, they didn't do a leach field. Some houses just had the holding tank, and when it's full it has to be pumped out. This is a very old house."

"There are people that do that?"

"That's what Smalley does. He'll send over Tom Elkins."

"Tonight?"

"I think I'd wait till everyone leaves."

"Let me ask you, is everyone peeing here?"

"Just the guys. The women's latrine is behind the barn. Who brought the deer jerky, by the way? I liked that."

Now that I was attuned to it, septic tanks came up in almost every conversation. Most of our upstate neighbors lived in old houses; they all had the same problems. It didn't matter if we were at dinner or at chance meetings in the grocery store. Somebody's lawn was always torn up for the world to see, the Smalley's truck was always in front of a neighbor's house.

"We just spent all night talking about human waste," Sue vented one night after a particularly graphic discussion. "Do we really have to talk about that at dinner?"

"No, of course not. We could talk about it before dinner. OK, how about after dinner? You're not giving me many options here. Anytime you're not in the room."

"I'll make it easy for you. Anytime I'm using the septic system, you can talk about it."

I made one exception to the no-visitors rule and invited Rob Corona up for the weekend. As I did every time we spoke. He had been in the hospital twice in the last year with pneumocystis pneumonia. His skin was peeling from his forehead. He was getting smaller; his head was starting to look too big for his body. He was taking AZT cocktails and couldn't keep them down. He was forty-three.

"I was wearing that brand-new Prada jacket that looks so good on me" he phoned. "I said I'd never spend that much money on a sports coat, but what can you do? It is a thing of great beauty. So, I'm standing at the curb at Fifty-third and Fifth one morning, waiting for the light to change, forty people crammed up around me. I said, 'Excuse me,' and vomited in the gutter. It was so sudden there wasn't time to do anything but open my mouth."

"That's a new way to meet people."

"Enchanted, I'm sure. At least I'm vomiting on Fifth Avenue. On Eighth Avenue, who'd notice?"

"You don't have to worry about crowds up here. We have plenty of room. Besides, what could be worse than breathing the air in New York City?"

"Not breathing it," he shot back. "Besides, there's nothing to do up there. Sue says you spend most of your time goofing."

"'Golfing.' You know damn well she said, 'Golfing.'"

"And the difference would be . . . ?"

· · ·

IT TURNS OUT we will *not* be eating the first corn and tomatoes of the season this week. The deer ate most of Sue's garden. But the deer are just the tip of the iceberg lettuce. Each night the woodchucks, the skunks, the raccoons, the mice, the voles, the chipmunks, and the squirrels feast on our cabbage and corn. They love to take one big bite out of each plant, then leave it to rot. The zucchini they won't touch. Zucchini we got plenty of. Of course, you can't give away zucchini.

The neighbors are full of good suggestions to keep the deer out of the garden. Abby said we should hang bags of human hair around the garden, Vardon Frasier said we should spread blood on the edges of the garden, Verbena said we should spread hot pepper around the garden.

I said, "Are we gardening, or practicing voodoo? Whatever happened to buying a fence?"

There were many other suggestions, most of them featuring some sort of impalement or decapitation, which seemed pretty extreme for the high crime of eating hobby farm lettuce.

WE WENT WITH Havahart traps for the smaller animals, wire cages that snare small animals without hurting them. You take the captured animal down the road and let it out to eat someone else's lettuce, instead of yours. It's the humane thing to do. Call PETA, please, we'll accept the award now.

You can debate the details, but do you really want to hang out with people who are *for* the unethical treatment of animals?

Over the next few weeks we caught and released many squirrels and chipmunks and began to live a new, happier, varmint-free life. It worked especially well on the rabbits, but the woodchucks proved to be pretty wily. We would catch one every now and then, but it was a rarity. It took a few weeks of experimenting to find out the best bait is cucumber peels.

One winter night we came home from a movie and in the glare of the high beams we spotted a rabbit in the trap on the front lawn. The poor thing was shivering with fear and cold. Rather than leave it out all night, Samaritan that I am, I put the trap in the trunk of the car and drove to our rabbit release spot, two miles away. If you don't take them far enough away they'll find their way back. I pulled off the road, opened the trunk, and put the trap on the ground. "Go on, buddy, go find a hole to crawl into tonight." The rabbit just sat there. I shooed it away, got back in the car, and made a quick U-turn. As I got back to the spot where I let our furry friend go, he jumped across the road and under the car. Splat! Here was a tale that Aesop must have missed—"The Flatlanders and the Rabbit."

For the deer, we decided to go with a wire fence. It was expensive, but we'll have to do it only once. But that wouldn't solve the woodchuck problem. They could dig under any fence. With them it turned into hand-to-hand combat, *mano-a-marmot*. Patrolling the perimeter one day, Sue spotted a woodchuck down by the barn and yelled for me to come help. I grabbed the first thing I could find—my 6-iron—and ran down there. We had the thing cornered and I started clubbing it. It was like something out of *Goodfellas*. Each smack made a sickening thump, but the thing wouldn't stop twitching. I didn't want it to suffer, but I couldn't seem to finish it off. Finally I came down with a mighty stroke right on its head. Woodchuck blood splattered all over me, my shirt, my pants, my face. But it stopped moving. Just then Vardon Frasier drove up. He looked at me and the shirt and the pants and the club, leaned out the window, and said, "I use a three-wood."

ON CERTAIN EVENINGS in August and September a full moon will rise that seems ten times bigger than the real moon, so big it's spooky, it takes up half the sky. Sometimes pumpkin orange, sometimes transparent yellow against the black silhouette of the spruce trees. A half hour later you look out the window and it is gone, replaced by a much less impressive, much smaller, grayer moon, the kind of moon you'd see in the city.

On certain mornings a cold front moves through and catches the early fog by surprise and freezes it. It is a rare thing; the air must be calm, the cold must come quick. And the sun, trying to burn it off, gives it an ethereal glow. We are inside a frozen cloud; it is like being inside a frosted white lightbulb. This is the dreaded pogonip Auntie Ellen told me to beware. Someday I'll have to ask her why.

COLUMBUS DAY IS cold and blue. Half the leaves are off the trees. There is no doubt that I will win today's pumpkin contest at Squire Danaher's. I really made an effort. All summer long I weeded it, watered it, picked squash bugs off it, pruned off the other little pumpkins so all the plant's energy would be focused into a single prize-winning fruit. My pumpkin has got to be the winner. It weighs 145 pounds and is eighty-five inches in diameter. It took both of us to lift it into the van. It is not a pretty thing. It looks as if you had taken 145 pounds of orange Silly Putty and dropped it down a flight of stairs. Of course, I'm just guessing about the weight because how can you weigh it? We tried a bathroom scale but the pumpkin is so big it covers the numbers.

THE SQUIRE'S LONG gravel driveway is lined with the cars of neighbors and friends. His driveway is kind of famous in Walleye. It's a long gravel road maybe four hundred feet long and, like many weekenders, he has Jesse Magrew clear it when it snows. One March it snowed thirty-eight inches in one twenty-four-hour period, unusual even here. It was so deep that it covered the thirty-six-inch-tall reflectors he had placed along his twisting driveway to guide the plow.

"It's not a worry," the squire says to Jesse. "I'll walk down the driveway and you'll follow me."

Jim Mullen

He starts walking and Magrew starts plowing. The squire looks behind him and spots the huge blade bearing down on him. It looks like it's inches away. He's terrified. So he struggles through the three-foot-deep snow to his left. The plow follows him. He's yelling, but Jesse can't hear him over the noise of the truck with the heater on and the windows closed. The squire lumbers to the right. Magrew follows him. Left, right, left, right. By the time they get to the garage, the squire is huffing and puffing and the sweat is dripping down his face. His five-acre front lawn looks like a Boy Scout knot-tying diagram.

It's up this maze way we go to drop off my blue-ribbon first-prize winner. The squire reaches into the car and pulls out my pumpkin with one hand.

"What happened?" he says. "You forget to water it?"

There are fifteen monster pumpkins sitting in the shade of his barn. Mine is the smallest by a half.

"Vardon Frasier's pumpkin weighed in at four hundred and three pounds. He found a spot on the Internet that told him all about giant pumpkins. But it split in the back of his pickup on the way over and is leaking juice. It may not weigh four hundred and three pounds at the final weigh-in."

NEIGHBORS HAVE SHOWN up with folding tables, lawn chairs, barbecue grills, and tons of food, most of it containing the mandatory Jell-O, Cool Whip, or miniature marshmallows. The squire is grilling the moose he shot last year on a hunting trip to New Mexico.

Mrs. Danaher is setting out the dishes everyone has
brought on the folding tables. Also from the old sod, when
she speaks, Mrs. Danaher sounds like she is singing.

"So, therrre you arrre!" she says to me. "I was thinking
about you just the otherrr day. I was at a matinee, have you
seen it I wonderrr, the name escapes me but it was about a
man and a woman who play carrrds and what rrreminded
me of you was that as we left the theater we rrran into one
of the poorrr unforrrtunates, a homeless man who said he
was out of work and could I spare any money. I said, 'Don't
worrrrrrrry, now, I've got a neighborrrr, Mrrr. Mullen, who
doesn't do a lick of work and he seems to be doing just fine,
so keep your chin up.'"

"But I . . ."

"Now stop flattering him, Mrs. Danaher," Sue jumps in.
"That kind of stuff will go straight to his head and then
there'll be no living with him."

Mrs. Danaher grabs a middle-aged couple passing on her
left. "Oh, I'd like you to meet the Tillotsons, Frrran and Wilson. They're staying in the guest barn this weekend. He's an
orrrthodontist, she's an activist shopperrr."

THE FARMERS STAND apart in a loose circle sporting
Agway and John Deere baseball caps and drinking Cokes.
Only flatlanders drink beer in the daytime. These guys all
have to go back to work in a few hours. They've all grown
up on farms, worked on farms, or owned farms their entire
lives.

Al is the first to speak, addressing the assembly with a well-thought-out word.

"Cutworms."

Vardon responds, "Root rot."

Doug nods seriously. "Crows."

One of the Tweedy brothers says, "Chinch bugs."

Not to be outdone, Walter Henderson says, "Scours."

Sam Musgrave's boy Sandy contributes "Broken back-loader." The round robin continues.

"Breeder."

"Rabies."

"Fungus."

"Lime."

"Leaf blight."

"Deer."

"Vet."

"Middlemen."

"Earworms."

"Raccoons."

"Whitewash."

"Taxes."

"Pigweed."

"Vaccinations."

"Dock."

"Armyworm."

"Skunks."

"Grasshoppers."

"Picking stone."

"Mending fence."

"Rust."

"Mold."

"Corn smut."

"Earwigs."

"Groundhogs."

"Beetles."

"Coy dogs."

"Silo gas."

"Mites."

"Root worm."

"Borers."

"Hired hands."

"Milk prices."

"Flatlanders!" Al has won with that one.

Of all the calamities that can befall a Catskills dairy farmer, flatlanders are the worst. Flatlanders are people who didn't grow up in the mountains. They do the strangest things. Like bicycling for exercise. How about doing some honest labor for exercise? Come milk a few cows and shovel some manure. That'll burn off some calories. Flatlanders go into town every day when they could wait and go once a month. Flatlanders read the *New York Times.* You won't learn how to milk a cow reading that. Flatlanders open the door in their bathrobes at eleven o'clock in the morning! Eleven in the G.D. A.M.! Can you imagine? Flatlanders get all palpitated when the power goes out. They move up here for the peace and quiet and then they complain about the dirt roads. "When are they gonna pave the road? When are they gonna pave the road!" When they pave the road you ain't gonna like that, neither. "How come there's so much traffic on the road?" they'll say. "How come there's so much traffic!" 'Cause we paved the G.D. road and made it easy for them to get here, you blathering fool! Flatlanders say things like, "I pay two hundred and fifty dollars a month for a parking space," and dry-clean their jeans. Flatlanders come up here and ask me if they can hunt on my land. Why is it I ain't got time to hunt on my land, but they do? Flatlanders! One day I milked my cows, fed the cows, did my chores, went up on the hill and baled seven hundred bales of hay and stacked it in the barn, missed supper because I had to mend some fence, was walking back to the barn for the second milking when a hunter comes down the hill and waves at me. "I'm so jealous of you," he says. "I wish I had the simple life." If I wasn't so tired I'da grabbed his gun and shot him on the spot. Flatlanders!

ABOUT FOUR IN the afternoon the squire announces it is time for the pumpkin weigh-off. The party will go on till midnight but the farmers must leave to get started on their chores. There are really only two pumpkins in contention—Vardon Frasier's and a weekender named Solomon Albanese's—and they are to be weighed last.

It turns out that my pumpkin was not the smallest, just one of the smallest. Vardon Frasier's was weighed on its pallet, then the pumpkin was rolled off the pallet so they could weigh the pallet by itself and subtract the difference. It had leaked twenty-seven pounds of juice since he first brought it in. Solomon's intact giant won at 394 pounds.

———

"WHERE IS MY leaf-raking coat?"

"It's in the mudroom, right where you left it."

I'm in the mudroom. You can't find a thing in here. Here's the jacket I wear in the spring when it's not that cold, but windy. A raincoat. A pair of insulated coveralls to go to the woodshed and back when it's twenty-two below. My winter jacket to go into town, a jacket for the snowmobile, a jacket for the bicycle. Work gloves, ski gloves, car gloves. Knit caps for the warmer summer days. A ski mask. A balaclava. A real, honest-to-God Billy Bob Thornton earflap special for the really cold days. My barn coat. My barn shoes. Some tall rubber muck boots for marshy bogs and spring flooding. A pair of lined boots for the snow. Then there's all Sue's jackets, gloves, boots, scarves, and barn clothes. Between the two of us it's impossible to find anything. Imagine living in a house with kids?

"It's not here."

"So wear something else."

"I don't have anything else."

. . .

WE WOKE TO the sound of gunshots. At first I thought I was back in the city. Then I remembered, you can't hear gunshots in the city over all the other noise. Maybe it's Al taking care of a woodchuck.

Farmers around here keep what they call a varmint gun near the back door. Usually an old .22 that looks like it's been around since the Great War, or a battered old shotgun. It's not the gun they hunt with, but it's the one they grab to shoot raccoons in the hayloft, noisy coy dogs up on the high fields, the occasional mangy fox, but mostly the woodchucks that dig holes in the fields that break the expensive farm equipment. But Sue won't have a gun in the house. "Too many accidents can happen." She is always looking at me when she says it.

There's another shot. It's not like Al to miss. Then we remember, deer season. As problematic as the deer have become, they're a minor annoyance compared to flatlanders who come to hunt them. It seems everyone on Long Island who can afford a safety orange vest and a six-pack is out in the woods shooting anything that moves and a lot of stuff that doesn't.

If they love the outdoors so much, if they're such woodsmen, why do they live on Long Island? Because the only thing they love about the outdoors is telling the guys at the office Monday morning that they peed against a tree. They don't mention the part where they got lost and the search-and-rescue squad had to go out and find them. They don't mention the fact that they shot a deer and didn't know how to field-dress it, so they left it to go get their buddies and when they finally found them—drinking beer around the dead cow they had bagged—they couldn't find their way back to the kill. They don't mention they left the carcass there to rot.

Yes, please, come back soon.

What if the situation were reversed? What if they issued hunting licenses to people in Catskill County to thin out the rats on Long Island?

It'd be ever so neighborly. We'd go down and walk across your front lawn with a big, deadly loaded weapon without asking permission. After all, the sign on your front porch that said, "No Rat Hunting," didn't have our names on it, so we thought it was OK. Then we'd shoot at your dog. He had no business looking so much like a rat. Or sometimes we'll just cruise down your street real slowly with a loaded shotgun sticking out the window. Then if we see something move we'll shoot at it from the moving car. Sure, it could be one of your kids, or one of your pets, but it could be a rat, too, and who wants them? We're doing you a favor, don't get so touchy.

There was a scene in Boody's store recently when a big guy dressed head to foot in brown-and-black camouflage smacked a brand-new shotgun down on the counter and asked Mr. Boody to show him how to load it. Boody took it away and told the guy if he wanted it back to bring the game warden with him. "Maybe instead of giving a million bad hunters a license to bag one deer," he said, "we should let ten thousand qualified hunters bag as many as they want."

———

$\mathcal{W}$E COME OUT of the Manhattan side of the Lincoln Tunnel. Where did all this trash come from? All the buildings that look so shiny from a distance look dingy and worn. There is the smell of leaky garbage bags left out in the sun on a hot day. As we pull up to the stoplight on West Forty-first Street a loud *thunk* comes from our car. Sue has hit the automatic door locks. Why didn't she do that while we were on Route 17? It's like an alarm signal for all the vagrants on the street who haven't been paying any attention to step forward. They approach the car in jerks and starts like some spoof of a cheesy George Romero ghoul-a-thon. She has to run the light into the honking traffic to escape. I feel myself turning into an out-of-towner. The city sidewalks aren't paved with gold, they're paved with gum. Or worse. The newly opened immigrant restaurants all look like they should be closed by the health department. I am turning into one of those horrible ex–New Yorkers who say nothing's the way it used to be, everything is dirty, everything is too expensive.

"Ten dollars to go from Fourteenth Street to Fifty-seventh Street! You've got to be kidding! When I lived here cabs were free. Once I

took a cab from midtown to LaGuardia and the driver gave me money! I left my wallet on the backseat and the driver brought it up to my office the next day. There was two hundred dollars more in it than there was when I lost it. And clean, my God, was this town clean. You could drop a cigarette butt and in seconds someone was along to clean it up. The bums wore ties. That's the way it used to be.

"You could see a Broadway show for a nickel. And that included dinner. And what is this thing called tipping? That's a new thing! Tipping? You're supposed to give a waiter extra money for doing the job he gets paid to do? I don't think so. You could win at three-card monte when we lived here."

THIS YEAR WE started driving to the city on Tuesday nights and driving back on Thursday. It was commuting in reverse. We were living at the farm and spending two days a week in Manhattan. It was an odd situation. Manhattan had become our weekend home. On Wednesday and Thursday we would run around trying to get all the things done that used to take us five days a week. We'd try to organize lunches and dinners with old friends and wonder why they couldn't make dinner at six thirty.

"Jim, I don't get out of the office till eight most nights," said Melissa. "What about nine thirty at Patria?"

Nine thirty? Is she out of her mind? "What about lunch?"

"On matinee day? I don't think so. Tell you what, meet me at Bombay Palace at three."

What was happening to me? I had broken the second rule

of doing business in Manhattan. The first rule of doing business in Manhattan is, Don't call anyone on Friday, especially in the summer. The real decision makers have left for their weekend homes Thursday night, leaving only the powerless and the "second homeless" in town. Calling someone on a Friday means you don't know this, and if you don't know this, you are obviously not worth talking to. The corollary is that if you are in town on Friday, don't answer the phone. If you answer your phone on a Friday, how powerful can you be? It is the perfect day to get some work done.

The second rule is, You can't go to lunch or dinner on Wednesday, matinee day. All the halfway decent places are crawling with busloads of suburban women who have come to see the worst musicals Broadway has to offer.

WE AIR-KISS at the restaurant, a giant Sikh leads us to a table and hands us off to three waiters.

Melissa is not wearing sensible shoes. Her navy skirt is skin tight, but it comes down to her ankles. She is wearing some kind of multicolored, ethnic, woven jacket over a simple white blouse, thirty or forty strand necklaces she has collected over the years around her neck. What out-of-the-way place could the jacket be from? Costa Rica? Thailand? Oaxaca? Her hair is black this week, and long. She is impossibly young, maybe twenty-four. Though we talk on the phone a lot about office business, it's the first time we've met face-to-face in six months.

"So, what have you been doing to keep busy upstate?"

"Watering the pumpkins, medicating the bees, checking the deer fence, putting up Posted signs, pruning back the raspberries, riding my bike, watching some cows. What's new here?"

"Well, today I cleaned out the twenty-eighth-floor refrigerator. I just found a turkey sandwich from someone who left us for *Teen People* a year and a half ago. Call me a clean freak, but if I don't do it, nobody will."

"For that you had to go to Yale?"

"Harvard, but thanks for reminding me. But that's the kind of thing you miss by not living in the city."

"But I didn't miss it. You just told me about it."

"You know what I mean. Don't you miss the interaction with people?"

"Yes. Yes, we do. We miss the interaction of saying, 'I saw this cab first.' We miss the interaction of saying, 'This stain wasn't here when I gave it to you.' We miss the interaction of opening the window and yelling, 'There are people trying to sleep up here, you know!' We miss the—"

"Boy, living in the country sure has mellowed you out. Where's all this anger coming from? You used to love Manhattan."

"I'm sorry, I'm going through some kind of phase."

There is something wrong with me. Like the deer, I think I may be an edge dweller. When I am in the city I want to be at the farm, on the farm I want to wave down a cab.

I'll see an ad for beautiful suit in a magazine and crave it. I don't wear suits anymore, I live in jeans and sweatshirts. I'll drool over pictures of computers with twice the power and speed of the one I have now. I can't type any faster, I can't think any faster, I can't write any faster, but I want it. There's a CD player down at Nobody Beats the Wiz that lets you load a hundred CDs. I'm thinking about buying it. So what that I can't find twelve CDs from Columbia House that I want for a penny. Where I would find a hundred CDs that I would want to hear? I still want to talk and think and act like I live in Manhattan even though I'm cured. Am I thinking this way because I'm older and wiser, or is it because I've stopped being a city person? Does Melissa think the way she does because she's young, or because she lives in the city?

"I SHOULD VISIT you up there. Where are you, again?"

"Three hours northwest of the city."

"How do you keep up with what's going on?"

"Oh, most days the noon stage brings a newspaper from the city. Course, it is a few months old by the time we get it. Is it true that no one wears spats anymore?"

Melissa says, "Either stay up there all the time or move back. But this in-between thing—it's not working."

She was right, I had changed too much. I used to think the more phone calls I got, the more meetings I had to attend, the thicker my Day-Timer, the fuller my life was. I've done a 180. Sometimes a whole day will go by without the phone ringing at all. My appointment book is the size of a check register. And that includes the address book. Most days there is nothing written in the calendar except an occasional note, like "Change cat's collar" or "Mom's birthday." Five calls is a hectic day.

WE TOOK THE final step. We stopped going into Manhattan altogether and rented the apartment on Christopher Street to a couple of lawyers. We moved all our furniture up to the farm. Now we have two of everything. Two frying pans, two dining room tables, two living room sofas, four phones, all the pottery, photographs, and books we'd accumulated over the years. The rooms are jammed with things that are too expensive to throw away, too ugly to keep. Even with a four-bedroom farmhouse, a basement, a huge barn, two greenhouses, and acres of land, we are running out of space. Soon we are going to have to have a lawn sale before the house caves in on itself.

ROB WORRIES THAT I will become a hopeless provincial by moving to the farm. Would I still be able to write from the middle of nowhere? Would I be able to keep my edge?

"I know you're not going to believe this, but they do have television upstate. At least, now that we have one of those little satellite dishes. We get the same shows you do. I get the *New York Times* and the *Washington Post* on-line. I read Liz Smith and Page Six every day—upstate! Imagine!"

"I'm sure," he condescended, "but you can't go to Broadway shows there. You can't go to the Metropolitan Museum of Art. You'll never eat shrimp and caper *tagliarini* again."

"If we ever want to see a show and have a fancy meal, we can always drive into town and stay with you."

"I don't think so. I'm not running a hostel here. If you're old and ugly, you're not sleeping in my guest room."

"No, if they're old and ugly they're sleeping in your bed."

"You're going to kill your career. You can't schmooze up there. Out of sight, out of mind."

"I like to think I get work because I have some talent."

"Oh, please. You make Larry King look like Saul Bellow. You're the Yanni of humor."

"Why I worry about getting more work with people like you out there blowing my horn every day, I'll never know."

"You can't tell me you don't miss the city."

"Yes, I do," I tell him. "I miss the smell of wino urine in the morning. I miss paying three hundred and fifty dollars a month for a parking space. I miss the ambulances, the fire engines, the car alarms, the horn honking, the drunken screaming winos, the Con Ed suction pumps, idling buses, reverse-gear beepers, the low-flying helicopters, the jackhammers, the rumbling gong of traffic going over those inch-thick metal plates they put over holes in the road. I miss telling people fascinating stories about how much I got gouged in the last twenty-four hours."

"You can make fun of Manhattan all you want, but tourists

from all over the world come here and are damn happy to pay through the nose for the privilege. I don't see them running up to the Catskills."

"Thank God. Let the tour buses go past your house."

"Besides, what do you guys do up there?"

What do we do? This is the question that makes us crazy. I know, I know, I used to ask it of my friends with weekend houses. The arrogance of the question now leaves me tongue-tied. Why would buying trinkets at Sharper Image, shopping on Madison Avenue, eating lunch at La Grenouille, getting Frédérick Fekkai hair be more important than watching the birds on the feeder, more important than watching Vardon make maple syrup, more important than watching Al spread manure? On whose scale does the one outweigh the other? Why is someone in Manhattan sitting at home in their apartment watching TV superior to me sitting in Walleye watching TV?

WHEN ROB ASKS, "What do you do?" what he really means is, "What is there to buy?" "Doing something" to me means mowing the lawn, writing a book, riding a bike, going golfing, going skiing, sitting out in the yard with Sue watching the cows graze on the squire's hay, watching my bees, growing giant pumpkins, yakking with our neighbors about how awful the weather is. To Rob and my city friends it means, "Where is there to shop? Where is there to eat? Where is there to go dancing? Where is the scene?"

With forehead-smacking clarity it came to me that a weekend in Walleye for Rob would be as horrible as a weekend in the Hamptons used to be for me. I changed my tack.

"What is there to do? Plenty. If you're lucky I might be able to get Al to let you drive his manure spreader. Then we could go into town and watch them put the mail in the boxes. Course, we'd have to get there before ten. What time do you get up nowadays? They're having a sale on sump pumps down at the Agway, we don't want to miss that. Doug's having his septic system pumped on Saturday. That's something to see. Come on up, it's all the stuff Disney wanted to do but couldn't."

There was a horrible, phlegmy cough from the other end of the line. Was I making him sicker, or was he trying to laugh? They were coming up with new things every day. How far away could a cure be anyway? A week? A month? I knew what I would miss about the city, and it wasn't restaurants and nightclubs.

Rob recovers his voice. "Now I know why the *Times* never mentions the Catskills in their Travel section. They're afraid people will run into you. Who would want to go to a place like that?"

IN THE COUNTRY, life changes with the seasons, its pace, its chores. In the summer, when the sun goes down at nine thirty, we stay outdoors as much as we can; neighbors honk and wave when they see us in the garden or out mowing the lawn or just sitting in the lawn chairs drinking sodas. Farmers on tractors are out cutting hay, planting corn, baling hay, working out where we can see them. Sometimes on a rare hot day or in a hot spell I'll complain about the heat, but I catch myself after a few minutes and remember how much I prayed for these days in the middle of the winter, when we would rarely leave the house, when there is no one to honk at, no one to wave to.

What is the difference between summer and winter on Wall Street? The buildings don't wave in the wind, they don't turn from brown to green to gold to gray; the windows don't fall out. The cabs are still yellow; people do the same thing they did last season. There is no dusk, there is no dawn. In the city I know when the moon is full only because there are more murders than usual. In Walleye I know when the moon is full because I can see it.

In the winter the sun comes up at nine and goes down at noon. We eat the food Sue canned in August, the pickles she made from the cukes she grew, the tomato sauce she made from the garden tomatoes. Every now and then Vardon drops by with some deer jerky or venison pepperoni, or a smoked wild turkey. When we need eggs I e-mail Lynn up the road and she'll leave three dozen out on her back porch for me.

IN THE MET there are several landscape paintings that, if they were ever to go on the market, would fetch tens of millions of dollars. Monets, van Goghs, Turners. It is only natural to crave them, they are works of great skill and beauty. What you would do with them when you got them home is another thing altogether. If you had an $82 million van Gogh hanging on your wall, could you ever watch your TV again without feeling silly? You're turning your back on an $82 million picture to watch *Jeopardy!*? And you'd need guards and insurance and climate-controlled air, and God forbid you should let sunlight touch it, and you'd need art experts to check it every now and then for wear and tear. Even if you were Bill Gates–rich it would be a bother and a bore.

On certain fall mornings, a heavy dew will cover the grass, the trees, the rooftops. Cobwebs you would never notice before—between tall stalks of grass in an alfalfa field, between branches in trees, between the close-together phone lines stretched from pole to pole—are covered with thick drops of water. On certain fall mornings the sunlight hits them at just the right angle and for a few minutes there are thousands of spiderweb prisms. In a few minutes the dew will evaporate, the angle of the sun will change, but for the seconds that it exists, it is a wonder. If a skillful painter could capture this scene, and if it were hanging in the Met in a big gilt frame, there would be a line around the block to see it. Ticket scalpers would have no problem getting hundreds of dollars for the "free" tickets. Guards would have to ask people to move along so other people could get a chance to see the most valuable painting in the world. I saw it this morning. There was no line. I was alone.

. . .

IT SNOWS AND blows so often it's not worth mentioning unless it stops. No snow, that would be news. Ice tracks cover the windows each morning, little Jackson Pollocks painted in frozen water.

The snow's been two feet deep on the ground for over a month. It started November 2 and it snows at least an inch or two every day. The snow plow got the mailbox today. I don't imagine we'll find it till spring. On the satellite I watched the weather reports on the city stations. There is an amazing similarity to them all. Panic.

> Oh my God! There's a chance of snow tomorrow. Get inside while you still can! Fill the bathtub with water, run to the store and buy six or eight months' worth of canned food. Some areas may get as much as two millimeters! Alternate side of the street parking has been canceled! Police are telling the public to keep their cars off the streets unless it's an absolute emergency. Don't shovel any snow, you could get a heart attack!

No wonder people panic if there is a threat of snow in the city. They might have to stay in the house and watch this kind of nonsense on TV all day, which must put a huge strain on the suicide hot line. We—we will throw another log on the fire and go to bed.

———

*W*E HAVE STARTED buying things in bulk now—toilet paper, rice, pasta—because we have the room and we can't go shopping every day, especially in the winter. There is so much stuff stored away we can't find it when we want it. We go out and buy ten more rolls of toilet paper, only to find we have two cases in the basement. Many times I'll buy a steak or a chicken for dinner, only to find Sue has three of them in the freezer. The mice, however, seem to have no problem finding things. We run down to the Agway to buy some hardware cloth to keep mice out of the pantry. It occurs to me that no one I know in Manhattan knows what hardware cloth is. "Some kind of industrial-strength chintz?" I can hear Rob guess.

On the way to the store, we pass a fly-covered deer carcass on the shoulder of the road. Sue looks at it unsympathetically and says, "One down, three hundred thousand to go."

Sue is wearing jeans, a ragged, frayed sweatshirt stained from years of use in the garden. I have on a filthy Carhartt barn jacket, paint-stained khakis stuffed into unlaced work boots.

A woman about forty, twenty pounds underweight, wearing a big, white, man's dress shirt, sleeves folded back to midforearm; high-fashion khaki pants; and some brand-new lace-up "paddock boots" she's found in a fancy gardening catalog, is tapping her foot at the checkout counter. Over her shoulder is a laundry-basket-sized Coach bag. She is blending in like Gwyneth Paltrow at a dirt track car race.

"Don't you have anything a little more, oh, faded? This rake looks so, so new! I'm really looking for something more 'country' looking," she explains to Darby, the clerk. "Can you show me what other colors they come in?"

Is this the future? Will they arrive in luxury SUVs and turn Walleye into some unpleasant, unwelcome Brigadoon that exists on summer weekends and then disappears again, not to be seen again until next Saturday? Will they complain about the bugs and fluffy supermarket bagels? I roll my eyes and think, Flatlander! Was I that thoughtless and silly when I first started coming up here on weekends? Must have been. Still am, probably.

Darby rings up our order and puts it on our account. "Need some signs for your lawn sale?" he asks. Neither of us show any surprise that Darby knows what we are thinking. "Maybe next week," I say.

THE APARTMENT ON Christopher Street worried me. What if the tenants wouldn't move out when they were supposed to? I'd heard stories about tenants who stop paying rent yet can't be kicked out for months. Years, even. Hell, *I* was a renter like that. When you're a renter it sounds like a great idea. Ripping off the capitalist pig landowners, man, I'm down with that. Now that I was a capitalist pig landowner it was keeping me awake at night. I dreaded getting a phone call one morning that the tenants had forgotten to turn off the bath water one day and then left for a three-week travel-adventure vacation in Kurdistan. Not only was our apartment destroyed, but so were the three underneath us. Everyone had hired lawyers and we were being sued by twenty-seven different people for damages, up to and including a woman who claimed she became a sex addict because of the leak caused by my tenants. So we made the decision to sell it. Rob Corona couldn't have been more wrong. We did not move up here five years after we bought the place. It was more like five and a half years. I so wish he were here to rub it in. We talked on a Monday, they found him unconscious on the floor of his loft on Wednesday, he died on Friday.

"BERT FERGUSON CALLED, the closing's in Brooklyn." I had not spoken to Ferguson since their visit.

"Why not Manhattan? The apartment is in Manhattan. Bert is in Manhattan. Our real estate agent is in Manhattan. Their lawyer is in Manhattan, the buyer is in Manhattan."

"The bank's in Brooklyn." To Sue this made sense, but not to me. We are selling the Christopher Street apartment we'd been renting out for the last year. It is the last step on our journey to the provinces. We would now rank several steps below matinee ladies on the tourist index, because at least they came to town once a week.

I don't care. I want to work less, not more. For the first time in my life I'm turning down jobs.

"I would love to write seven hundred and fifty words for you on ATM cards for children," I tell the caller, "but I got a ten o'clock tee time."

"Five hundred words. And I'll give you another five hundred dollars."

"I live on a farm. What am I going to do with another five hundred dollars? Buy more peace and quiet? I'm a recovering workaholic. If I ever go near work again I may not be able to stop."

BERT FERGUSON TRAVELS a lot on business, to the West Coast for clients, to Europe and Japan. He grew up in Manhattan and still lives on the Upper East Side. He can remember every meal he's ever eaten and the wine he had with it. He knows the obscure back streets of Paris and London. Sue says we have to give him a ride to the closing.

"He can't take a cab?"

"He won't. He's never been to Brooklyn. He's afraid he won't find the place."

"You're kidding? You're *not* kidding. He's forty-five years old and he's never been to Brooklyn? It's across the river, for Christ's sake. That's like living in Nebraska and saying you've never seen corn. I can't wait to tell Trude."

"We have to pick up Trude, too."

"Stop it."

Our real estate agent has never been to Brooklyn, either? She grew up in Greenwich Village.

"You're telling me she's never, ever been over the bridge to Brooklyn? My God, that's crazy. They've never been to Junior's or BAM or Coney Island or the Botanic Garden?"

"That's the way it is. Now, come help me put the backseat in the van."

"Why? We've got four seats. What do we need two more for?"

"The buyer and his lawyer."

"Let me guess: live in Manhattan, never been to Brooklyn."

"No, smarty-pants, their lawyer's from Tarrytown. He's taking the train to Manhattan and we'll pick him up and take him to Brooklyn."

IT WAS SLOWLY dawning on us that we were not the provincials in this story. In the car ride out, Ferguson is telling us about his last trip to Paris, his last meal at Tallivent. He is describing it in mouthwatering detail.

"And what did Beverly have?"

"Herbal tea and grape peels." It seems after her lapse at the Big Pig, Beverly has adopted an even stricter regime. No gluten. No dairy. No meat. No eggs. No salt. No soy. That doesn't stop her from asking the waiter about every item on the menu before telling him exactly what ingredient prevents her from ordering it (as if he cares), finally deciding that the only thing she can have is tea and fruit peelings. Then she sits and watches Bert eat. How much fun can two people have? Most of the time she sends the tea back. She does, however, tip 20 percent.

THE OFFICE FOR the closing is in the shadow of the Verrazano Narrows Bridge, along the entrance to New York Harbor. It is football weather, bright and crisp, the leaves off the trees. We park across the street from Fort Hamilton Park, a narrow strip of riverfront greenery. The vast bridge takes up a quarter of the view—the harbor, Staten Island on the far shore, the Statue of Liberty, the distant skyline of Manhattan take the rest. It has a San Francisco–like quality and I wonder what houses with a similar view would cost there. A fortune, no doubt. And only the wealthiest and most cosmopolitan folks would have them. But this is a middle-class neighborhood. Most of the residents are not at work, but in Florida for the winter. Row after row of postwar six-story apartment buildings line the street. No one is out, no children, no adults.

"Shouldn't someone stay with the car?" asked Trude.

"Don't you have the Club?" asked Ferguson.

"I brought pepper spray," said the buyer.

"Put a sign in the window that says, 'Radio Already Stolen,'" suggested the buyer's attorney.

A gray-haired, sinewy-legged jogger went by. Instinctively, Sue and I waved. He waved back.

"Do you know him?" asked Trude.

"What difference would that make?"

"Are you trying to get us killed?" asked the buyer.

"He was casing your van. I've got a cell phone, do you want me to call 911?" asked Bert.

"We are a little early," I said. "Why don't we go take a walk in the park and kill ten minutes?"

"Not even with a gun."

———

Minutes later we no longer own a Manhattan apartment, we have no riv vw, no wbfp. The three-hour ride home seems very fast, we are never stuck in traffic. We can go forward, we can go left or right, and every now and then we'll go back. But it's sinking in that the next time we want to see a Broadway play or a special show at the Met or eat grilled pompano on a bed of wilted mesclun we'll have to rent a room.

For the first time since the pumpkin contest, we drove past Vardon Frasier's ramshackle compound. There were bulldozers and backhoes and frontloaders everywhere. The wall of hubcaps was going under the dozer's blade the very moment we drove past. Vardon, his hair pulled back in a ponytail, was standing at a makeshift sawhorse table with a guy who looked like he just robbed an Eddie Bauer store. Every garment he was wearing that wasn't leather was trimmed in leather. Even his glasses. When he saw our car, Vardon waved us over.

"We're just going over the els of the new place," he announced. "This is my architect, Harrison Fiddich. He worked on Olan Obert's penthouse, maybe you saw it in last month's *Architectural Digest?*" Sue says, "No, have you ever had anything in *Reader's Digest?*"

The house was going to be a giant log cabin. Vardon started showing us the mock-ups.

"They made the whole thing in Vermont, then took it apart and shipped it here piece by piece. Each log was carved by hand and they fit together so well that we don't have to plaster in between them. The sheer weight of the wood keeps everything tight. All electrical wiring and plumbing holes were drilled before they were reconstructed so that no holes are visible. Each light switch, each socket, each vent will sit perfectly flush into the wood.

"The ballroom will be tiled in brown leather and they made three chandeliers out of the deer racks I've got over the years. This will be kitchen, here are the servants' quarters and the bathrooms."

The second and third floors had balconied bedrooms that overlooked the ballroom from the inside, and dormered windows overlooking the entire valley. The shower in the master bath will have a waterfall built of stone gathered from the property and using springwater from his own well. There will be his and her sinks, his and her toilets, his and her bidets.

The kitchen was a rustic throwback—a commercial Garland range, matching Sub-Zeros, a butcher-block island with a temperature-controlled wine cellar. There is a built-in Tuscan stone oven for home-baked bread.

"Neat, huh?"

"Yes," says Sue, "just like the pioneers."

Though Catskill County may have more charming stone fences than any county on the planet, laborers were busily building new ones all over the property. As George S. Kaufman said about Moss Hart's Bucks County farm, "It's what God would have done if he had the money."

"I didn't know you could make this kind of money milking cows."

"Du-uh. Of course you can't. Remember that joke you told me at the pumpkin contest? About the guy who was going into debt betting the horses? The one where the guy lost so much money that his bookie wouldn't give him any more credit because he knew the guy could never pay it back? The bookie says, 'Face it, you're just no good with the ponies. Why don't you bet on something else? Like football.'

"'But I can't,' says the bettor. 'I don't know anything about football.'

"All I kept thinking was if you change the word 'bettor' to 'farmer,' you've got me. I sold the herd right after I lost the pumpkin contest, took the money, and bought stock in eBay. You know, I've been going to auctions down at Sam Musgrave's for years and when I heard about this on-line auction deal, well, it just made good sense to me. I made more

money in six months than all the farms on this road put together made in forty years. Harrison likes the area so much
he's thinking of telling his friends like Olan to buy property
up here. Hey, I'll talk to you later. I want to see Harrison's
plans for turning the barn into a guest house." As we back
away he says, "Call me!"

We got back in the car. Without thinking, we both said, "I
need a cigarette."

WELL, NO PLACE is perfect. Hell, we're not even close.
A new Chinese restaurant opened in Trout Creek, a big
event up here. They serve cheeseburgers and milk shakes.
And huge portions of barbecue beef. There are no chop-
sticks, no little packets of mustard and duck sauce, no faded
pictures of *moo goo gai pan* hanging over the counter. The
only thing remotely Chinese about the place is that you get a
fortune cookie at the end of the meal, which, as everyone
knows, is an American idea. Mine said, "Smile and the world
smiles with you." I said to the guy behind the counter, "This
is not a fortune, it's an aphorism."

"Flatlander!" muttered the Asian man behind the counter.

Author's Note

The Catskill Mountains make up part or all of eight New York State counties, but there is no Catskill County in New York State, nor a town called Walleye. Any similarity between real persons and the characters in this book (not related to me by marriage) is wishful thinking.

There were six hundred working dairy farms in our non-fictional county when we started coming to the Catskills in 1987. There are fewer than two hundred today.

Thanks

To Cindy Grisolia, Kim Hastreiter, David Hershkovits, Jim Kerr, Maggie Murphy, Barbara O'Dair, Mary Peacock, and Hal Rubenstein for their help and encouragement over the years.

To Gene and Norman, who heard this long before anyone and laughed in all the right places.

To Jessica Shaw, for lighting this particular candle.

To my upstate neighbors for their generosity.

To Lisa Bankoff and Geoffrey Kloske, for their patience and skill.

To Jim Seymore at *Entertainment Weekly*, for paying me to live the life of Reilly.

And more than anyone, to Susan Mahoney Mullen, who had to live through the not-so-funny parts as well.

Jim Mullen has written the "Hot Sheet" column for *Entertainment Weekly* for ten years. His humor has also appeared in the *New York Times*, *New York* magazine, and the *Village Voice*. He was a contributor to *Paisley Goes with Nothing* by Hal Rubenstein.